151
Quick Ideas

for Delegating and Decision Making

151
Quick Ideas

for Delegating
and
Decision Making

Robert E. Dittmer and
Stephanie McFarland

CAREER
PRESS
Franklin Lakes, NJ

151 Quick Ideas for Delegating and Decision Making
Edited by Dianna Walsh
Typeset by Gina Talucci
Cover design by Jeff Piasky
Printed in the U.S.A. by Book-mart Press

To order this title, please call toll-free 1-800-CAREER-1 (NJ and Canada: 201-848-0310) to order using VISA or MasterCard, or for further information on books from Career Press.

The Career Press, Inc., 3 Tice Road, PO Box 687,
Franklin Lakes, NJ 07417
www.careerpress.com

Library of Congress Cataloging-in-Publication Data
Dittmer, Robert E., 1950-
    151 quick ideas for delegating and decision making / by Robert E. Dittmer and Stephanie McFarland.
              p. cm.
Includes index.
    ISBN-13: 978-1-56414-961-9
    ISBN-10: 1-56414-961-7
        1. Decision making. 2. Delegation of authority. I. McFarland, Stephanie, 1968- II. Title. III. Title: One hundred fifty-one quick ideas for delegating and decision making. IV. Title: Delegating and decision making.

HD30.23.D62 2007
658.4'03--dc22

                                                                2007025101

Contents

How to Use This Book

Every quick idea in this book is tested and true. They come from the collected experiences and wisdom of literally hundreds of people—well beyond just the authors. And they are presented here to help you learn how better to make high quality decisions and to learn the best practices in delegating.

The book is designed to be consumed piecemeal—that is, in small bites. So don't try all of these ideas all at once. Some should logically follow others—it will be obvious to you as you read through the book. So, read the book quickly through to gain a quick impression of the ideas here. Then start picking out those that seem to you to be immediately helpful and try them out. They are the ones that can make a quick difference. Later, review the book again and try some additional ideas.

Of course, some of these ideas are in sequence and those will be obvious and will make logical sense to you when you read them. Later, go back and review the others routinely and pick a few more to try. And so on...

So, on first read, label the ideas you read as:

◆ Implement these ideas now.

◆ Review thee ideas in a month

◆ Review these ideas later

◆ Pass this idea on to _____.

11

If you have a staff, involve them in this process. Get their reactions and thoughts. Perhaps even invest in additional copies of this book and distribute them to others who work for you for discussion and professional development. Get more than just yourself involved if you can.

Every 90 days or so, revisit the book for some new ideas or techniques. As you situation changes you may well find ideas that are usable that you discounted earlier.

Remember, all of these ideas and concepts are proven techniques. Proven by research and other professionals around the country and around the world. They have worked for others and they can work for you!

Introduction

Congratulations on an excellent decision: buying this book.

Whether you are just starting out in management, are a long-time seasoned leader, or are working your way to that first manager role, this book is right for you. It's filled with quick, simple, yet compelling tips on how to make decisions more effectively, and how to implement them through delegation.

Making decisions and delegating are the two most important responsibilities of management. Yet, they are the two most difficult skills to master. After all, managers are learning how to make decisions and delegate on the fly as they hurry their way through, day to day, just trying to get it all done.

151 Quick Ideas for Delegating and Decision Making pulls together tips and insights in one easy-to-use guide that can help you become a leader among leaders.

In this book, you will learn how to know when it's time to make decisions by consensus, and when it's time to go solo. You'll also learn how to develop a strategy for making better decisions, time after time, and how to analyze decisions before they are made and after they are implemented. You'll learn how to go "mindless" when decisions become too overwhelming.

Yet *151 Quick Ideas for Delegating and Decision Making* goes one step further. It also gives you insights on how to better implement your decisions, and how to influence people and develop your employees to get better results. For example, you'll learn how to overcome the biggest stumbling blocks to delegating, such as giving up power, facing your fear of failure, and letting go of perfection. And it also gives you proactive tips on how to leverage your management style, how to determine which employees are best for what jobs, and how to delegate sideways and upwards to colleagues and superiors.

In short, this book is an excellent guide—filled with quick tips that are easy to digest and fun to learn—to help you set up your own system for creating opportunities, and succeeding at them day after day.

1

What Is a Decision?

Yes, this sounds like a stupid question. But wait—it isn't, really. We often think we are making decisions when what we are really doing is simply making choices. Decision making is a management tool designed to be much more than just selecting from some choices.

While there are often choices in decision making—at least one hopes there are—those choices must be analyzed in terms of outcomes and consequences. That is what makes decision making a management process in any organization. It is the focus on achieving desired outcomes that is important.

Thus, decision making is a process of analyzing alternatives to reduce uncertainty about achieving a desired outcome. Of course, along the way, we must always be concerned with unintended consequences, but more about those later.

So, decision making for managers is the identification of alternative solutions to problems, challenges, and opportunities; the analysis of those alternatives; and the selection of the alternative most likely to achieve the desired outcome with the best affect on the organization. There! How's that for a

Assignment

Review your role in your organization and think about the decisions you commonly make. Review your process for making those decisions. Determine if you have made those decisions in the past based on desired outcomes.

definition? Pretty simple, right? Well, maybe not. We are going to spend another 92 ideas on this process called decision making. It's not simple, if you want to get it right, that is.

Epilogue

The quality of a decision is really based on a number of factors, but the process is extremely important. So, let's get it right!

Decisions as Remedies

As we examine decision making, we can view the process as one with two potential goals: first, to fix problems or challenges we have identified, and second, to make decisions that advance the organization.

Probably the most common decisions are made to remedy a problem inside the organization. We are constantly faced with these in life. For example, our son brings home a bad report card, so you make a decision

Assignment

Think about some of the recent decisions you have made in your personal and professional life and identify which are remedies, or decisions to fix something. Think about those circumstances. We'll come back to those later.

to require him to study and do his homework every night before he can watch TV, surf the Internet, or play a video game.

You have identified a problem and created a solution to the problem—a remedy, so to speak. In doing so, you probably evaluated a number of different alternative solutions and arrived at this one.

We do the same kind of decision making in our organizations all the time.

Epilogue

Solutions to problems are the most common decisions we make in life, and are often the ones we are most practiced at accomplishing; but there are others.

3

Decisions as Avenues to Progress

The other major kind of decision is one in which you must determine how to take advantage of an opportunity, or how to move the goals and objectives of an organization forward. These are quite challenging, and demand quality decision-making skills.

As managers, we are often called upon to make decisions to move the organization forward—to increase the chances of

Assignment

Similar to the previous assignment, think about some of the decisions you have made recently in your professional life and identify those designed to advance the cause, to achieve progress for the organization.

achieving stated goals and objectives. We normally equate the achievement of these goals and objectives as progress, and that's what managers do: they make progress, achieve goals and objectives, and ensure the constant success of the organization.

Achieving these goals almost always requires quality decisions made from a wide variety of alternatives and in a broad range of settings and circumstances. The decisions are often complex, involve many people, have significant consequences and ultimately determine the extent of success or failure of the organization.

How's that for decision making as a management function? Feel the pressure? Stress building up?

Well, it doesn't have to. There are tried-and-true ways to handle these decisions, and that's what this section of the book is about.

Epilogue

Decision making to promote the organization's success is what being a manager is all about. Good decision-making skills will help make you a good—or even great—manager.

4

Making the Decision: Is It Yours to Make?

Here's the first decision you have to make: Do you really have to make this decision?

Sounds like a dumb question, but it's not! Your first task in any decision-making situation is to make certain it is your responsibility to make this decision. Sometimes we all have a

Assignment

Think about decisions that have been made in the past that clearly were made in the heat of the moment by the wrong person. Did the results turn out badly?

tendency to rush into a situation and "fix it." Often, that calls for some decision making. Yet, if we took the time to think about it, the situation may require a decision by someone else, not us. How to decide?

Start with the situation. Does it require a decision right now? Are you the person who logically should make the decision? If it isn't a crisis or emergency, would you still be the one to make the decision? If the answers to these questions are yes, then make the call.

If, however, the answers are no, then it may be someone else's decision to make. Next questions: Are they there to make the decision? Is there time for them to do so? If not, perhaps you will need to make the decision for them.

If time is not of the essence, then consult with anyone involved to determine whose decision it is to make.

Epilogue
Don't make decisions you don't have to or shouldn't. They never turn out right.

5

A Key Question: Why Are You Making This Decision?

There are those managers who just love to make decisions. It provides confirmation of their purpose in the organization, and it often gives them a sense of power and authority. It is personally and professionally rewarding to them to be able to make decisions.

> ### *Assignment*
>
> Think about these questions. They are not posed lightly. Think about situations you may find yourself in where your personal stake in the outcome might be a problem.

Yet, it is always important to remember that the ability and authority to make decisions are not a right, but a responsibility. It is an important role and function of management, and should not be taken lightly, or undertaken for personal reasons or ends.

Just as importantly, it is critical to ensure that you are the correct person to make the decision. Ask the following questions before undertaking the decision-making task:

- ◆ Is this my decision because I am responsible for the outcome?

- ◆ Is this my decision because I am responsible for the people involved?

- ◆ Is there someone else who might be more qualified to make the decision?

- ◆ Is this a decision my boss should make?

Finally, ask yourself if you have a personal stake in the outcome. If you do, while it may still be your decision to make, you should identify your position and try to set it aside so you can make a rational and objective decision—not one influenced by your own motivations.

Epilogue

Making decisions for the wrong reasons may well turn out alright, but they might turn out badly as others discover the decision was made for personal reasons.

6

Decisions to Save Face

Sometimes we find ourselves in situations where we are tempted to make a decision that affects others because we made a mistake, and are trying to make up it. We are trying to "save face," saving our personal reputation from damage.

If this is the only reason for making the decision, it is a bad one. Decisions should be made for the good of the organization and its members, not to help one manager save his or her reputation from damage.

Assignment

Remember when you have seen others decide something only so they can cover for their own mistake. How do you feel about that?

If you find yourself thinking about whether to do something or not, solely for the purposes of making up for—or covering for—a previous mistake, don't do it. Stop at that point. If you've screwed up, take your lumps and move on. There will be other times to shine.

Epilogue

So, do you want to be one of those people? Probably not.

7

Decisions to Gain Prestige

Here is another questionable motivation for making a decision: If the reason you think you have a decision to make is because you will gain in reputation or in influence—prestige—then the real outcome of the decision is not for others or for the organization, it's for you.

These situations almost never work out to your advantage. You may think you have a good reason for the decision, but most will see

Assignment

You've seen others do this before you. You didn't respect them then.

through your rationalizations and see it for what it is: an attempt to improve your prestige in the organization.

Resist these impulses to make a decision just because it's good for you.

Epilogue

Don't become one of those you have criticized in the past.

8

Decisions to Fit In

This is another decision you are tempted to make not because the organization needs it, but because you need it, which is always a questionable motivation. The desire for new managers to fit in with their new peer group of other managers is strong—and normal.

However, there are many more ways to begin the fitting-in process than by making decisions for that purpose alone. Again, the people who are affected by that decision will immediately recognize your motivation and think less of you for it. And your new peer group will also see the same thing; your credibility and capability will be damaged.

Instead, to fit in, become a resource to other managers. Become someone they can count on for help and advice. Get to know them and let them get to know you.

Assignment

Recall others who have made decisions just to be "one of the team." You didn't respect it then, and others will not respect it from you.

Epilogue

Fitting in with a new peer group involves relationship building, not decision making.

9

Decisions to Get Promoted

Probably the worst motivation for making any decision is the personal, self-aggrandizing motivation of making a decision in such a way as to position yourself for a promotion. This usually means a decision that benefits you, but not others. You've seen this: A manager reorganizes his department just to demonstrate he has ideas rather than because the department will be more efficient or effective after the reorganization.

Assignment

Resist the motivation to make decisions for personal advancement.

There are two good reasons to reject this motivation for a decision. First, it's a poor excuse to make a decision. As a manager, you are charged with making decisions to improve outcomes for the organization—not yourself.

Second, those you think you will be impressing will recognize the motivation and will not value it. You may think they will not notice—but they certainly will. Remember, you did when you saw things like this happen!

Epilogue

Decisions for personal motivations usually backfire.

10

Is It Soley Your Decision to Make?

Not every decision requires a sole decision maker. Many, especially in business and industry, require a number of very informed and involved decision makers to collectively make the best decision for the organization. Decisive people, perhaps like you, tend to want to "make things happen." But sometimes it's best to either pass the decision to someone else who may be more appropriate, or, even more common, involve others in the decision.

> **Assignment**
>
> Review the decisions you have made or participated in making in the past. How many were sole decisions by yourself or others and how many were group or collaborative decisions? Use this set of experiences as a guide.

At other times, expediency will suggest that the decision should be made in consultation with other managers or perhaps with your boss—all of whom may well have an important stake in the outcome(s). Consider those players, and the circumstances, before undertaking the decision alone.

But you need to determine that based on the evidence. What is the nature of the decision? Who will it affect? Will it affect others besides those I am responsible for supervising?

Will it affect processes conducted by others? These kinds of questions will help you determine who should be involved in the decision process.

Epilogue
Remember that a shared decision is often not only better received, but also better implemented.

11

Do You Need to Share the Decision With Someone Else?

Seems like a simple questions, doesn't it? To share or not to share. Yet, it is not always that easy to tell. If you have analyzed the situation as we have already suggested, you know who needs to be involved. But do you know whether they need to share in the decision process or just be consulted?

We're back to some of those earlier questions. Who should be involved and why? The *why* will suggest if they need to be a co-decision maker. Sometimes there is just one other person

Assignment

Review past decisions and consider those that were consultative versus consensus. Why were they consultative and not consensus, or vice versa? Your own past experiences will be important here.

with an important stake in the outcome of the decision. When that is the case, consider consulting and sharing the decision process and outcome with him or her.

Sometimes there are many with a stake in the process or outcome. In those cases, you will need to decide (yes, another decision) whether you will consult and then make a decision, or whether you will work toward a consensus.

Each of these options is different, and requires slightly different processes and concerns.

Epilogue

Consulting versus consensus can make a real difference in the success of the outcome of your decision.

12

Consulting the Key Players

Once you have identified the need to make a decision and consult with key people, you need to make certain you have correctly identified the right players. A rule of thumb is that anyone who will be affected by the decision should be consulted. If their processes will be affected, consult them. If their business outcomes will be affected, consult them. This applies to other managers as well as to your own work team.

When consulting, make sure you convey to them that you are only doing that—consulting. You will make the decision, but you are asking for their input and recommendations. Never imply that they are part of the decision-making process. When you consult, you are clearly seeking input, not partners in the decision.

> **Assignment**
>
> Practice a few lines akin to this example. Write them down so you can retrieve them as needed. Make certain they clearly indicate you will be making the decision, and you are asking only for input.

Here's one way to do this: "Hi, Frank, I'm trying to decide whether to move our Task A from Office A to Office B. As I make my decision, I'm asking any key players, like you, what the affect might be from your perspective." A statement like this clearly asks for input, yet just as directly indicates you will be making the decision.

Epilogue

Consult anyone whose processes or outcomes will be affected by your decision.

13

Do You Need a Consensus?

Consensus is a decision-making technique that uses all of the resources and the participation of an entire group. That could be a group of managers, or it could be a group of workers. Consensus always requires more time to make the decision than a simple managerial decision. It also is not a democratic vote.

Consensus involves compromise by the group making the decision. Not everyone can always get everything he or she wants. Often, your role as a manager is to mediate and moderate the process to an effective conclusion: the decision.

More often than not, consensus will require the participants to negotiate an acceptable solution that requires trade-offs. Not everyone will get what he or she wants. What you are looking for is a final product that everyone can live with,

which actually achieves your goal. The result is a reasonable decision that everyone in the group can accept.

Epilogue

Consensus decisions are difficult to manage and obtain, but often provide the best results through time. Your task is to manage the process effectively and efficiently.

14

Is Consensus Decision Making Right for Your Situation?

Of course, deciding when consensus decision making is appropriate is the key to using this mechanism best.

Consensus decision making is best used when there is a clearly identifiable group or team to make the decision. The boundaries of the group need to be clear, such as a normal work team with a clearly established membership and common goals and objectives, or a management team that routinely meets to collaborate—not an ad hoc group of people just brought together, which just ends up being consultation.

The situation needs to be right as well. Never use consensus for personal actions. That's a manager's job, pure and simple. Never use consensus for determining equipment purchases, product development decisions, budget decisions, or similar situations.

Consensus decision making is best when the team members, or participants, have a real stake in the process or the outcome, or both: a work team deciding how most effectively to achieve a goal or objective; a management team deciding how best to integrate new processes or procedures that affect everyone; or a group of workers deciding how best to change a process to increase efficiency.

All of these are good situations for consensus decision making. Remember, however, that the manager's role is to facilitate this process.

> **Assignment**
>
> Review consensus decision-making situations you have participated in, and determine why they were or were not appropriate situations for a consensus decision. We often learn best from our own experiences.

Epilogue

Consensus decision making is hard work. But the potential rewards are significant. Make certain you choose wisely.

15

When Consensus Is the Answer

Studies and experience have demonstrated time and time again that consensus decisions are almost always the best and highest quality decisions; they often produce the best outcomes.

This is based on what we know about people's behaviors and motivations. If they are involved in the decision process, they are invested in its result. Behaviorally, they recognize they are at least partly responsible for the success of the decision's outcome.

People work harder and more energetically to execute an idea or decision they had a role in making, and this almost always results in significantly improved outcomes.

Use consensus decision making when you have plenty of time to create the decision, and when you have a clearly identifiable and cohesive group of people to participate in the process. Use consensus decision making when quality is more important than time. Quite frankly, this should be most of the time.

Assignment

Recall the consensus decisions you have participated throughout the years. Did you feel better about that decision than others you were not a participant in? Were you more likely to work harder at that implementation than others?

Epilogue

Consensus decisions almost always result in higher quality decisions and immediate group acceptance and execution.

16

When It's Not

So when do you not use consensus decision making?

An authoritarian decision is appropriate under some circumstances where consensus is either not possible or not practical. This sounds negative, but it doesn't have to be. An authoritarian decision is one made by someone with the "authority" to make the decision.

There are two primary factors that may dictate whether or not an authoritative decision is appropriate: time and politics.

When time is of the essence, an authoritarian decision is best made. Getting groups together, discussing the process, and arriving at a consensus decision takes time—time you don't always have. If you are in a crisis or an emergency, don't go for a consensus decision, make one yourself.

Organization politics can sometimes be a barrier to a good or practical decision. Not every organization is a smoothly running machine. Sometimes internal divisions are significant and divisive. If it is likely that internal groups will polarize around specific positions and be unbending, then it becomes almost impossible to obtain a good consensus decision. So, when the internal organizational politics of the situation indicate many different and widely divergent factions will preclude a quality decision, use authoritarian style.

Assignment

Recall the decisions you have seen made in the authoritarian style. Evaluate the circumstances and the outcomes.

Epilogue

Authoritarian decisions are often expedient decisions. They aren't always the best decisions, just the best decision time and circumstances will allow.

17

Know Your Decision-Making Style

Each of us tends to have a favorite decision-making style. After all, we have been making decisions our entire lives! Most of them have been personal decisions about our own lives, but they are decisions nonetheless and we are comfortable making them.

However, our personal decision making styles may work well for us, but not for our organization. Beware of applying your personal style to your organization. It may not work very well.

For example, some of us are "thinkers." We want to think through a problem or challenge and arrive at a decision based on evidence, facts, and so on. Others of us are "feelers." We make decisions emotionally based on how we feel about a situation, problem, or challenge.

Assignment

Evaluate your personal decision-making style. How do you make personal decisions? Is this style appropriate for your organizational decisions as a manager?

Quite frankly, neither of these styles alone are appropriate for an organizational decision. Certainly thinking and analyzing are fine techniques, and we all have emotions that are applicable to most situations. But using these alone is inappropriate. Just thinking about a problem does not get you input from others, and emotions should not play a role in organizational decisions.

Epilogue

Just thinking and feeling are too simple and not inclusive enough for quality organizational decision making.

18

Simple Decisions

Not all decisions are complex or require sophisticated negotiating skills. Some are really simple, and you can make quick work of them.

The quickest decisions are those that already have established guidelines and policies. For example, let's say you want to hold a client luncheon to showcase your latest product. If you know you can spend budget dollars for it, and you have the money to do so, then you've met the two criteria to finalize the decision. In short, you went, you saw, you conquered—you're done!

The point is, don't waste time and energy on thinking about simple decisions. And don't waste time battling

---

Assignment

Take the win-win approach, even in the simplest decisions, and you will end up with more energy, goodwill, and thinking power to tackle the bigger fish.

---

over small decisions in group decision making, either. Concede where you can, make your pitch, and then let the chips fall where they may. In other words, don't pull out a bazooka to kill a mosquito.

Epilogue

If the parameters for making the decision are clear-cut, then your decision should be clear and simple as well.

19

What's the Problem?

So, how do we start making decisions?

We start at the beginning, as with everything else, and we try to figure out the problem. The first step is to recognize that a problem actually exists. Sometimes they are large problems and simply cannot be ignored. They "slap you upside the head." Other times, problems are more subtle, and you need to be observant and analytical.

Assignment

To practice this technique, think about some of the problems you have faced in the past and create a simple declarative sentence that describes the problem.

Once we have decided there is a problem (or a challenge or an opportunity), we have to clearly define it. It could be a process problem, a customer service problem, a manufacturing problem, or a personnel policy problem.

First, try to define it with a simple declarative statement. For example, if customers are returning a specific product 35 percent of the time, clearly state the problem this way: "Our customers have problems with Product X at least 35 percent of the time; we know this because they are returning it to us."

Okay, that's pretty clear. You have a problem with a product. Customers are returning it. There must be something wrong with either the product or the presentation of it. This requires a solution, and a decision about that solution will be required. Now you need to begin researching the problem to find out more about it.

Epilogue

Understanding the problem begins with stating the problem clearly.

20

Covey Has It Right: Start With the End in Mind

If you know where you want to go, you're halfway there. That's the concept best-selling author Stephen Covey describes when he talks about starting with the end in mind. Suggesting that you work in a backward direction may sound odd, but it's absolutely necessary to move you forward in the right direction.

Starting with the end in mind is a perfect principle to apply in decision making. In fact, it's the founding premise for MBO, or "managing by objective." The term *objective* often gets thrown around like a piece of strategic code, but it simply means "the end result."

For example, all parents want to raise their children to become self-sufficient. Starting with the end in mind, in this case, means defining what self-sufficient means, picturing it, perhaps describing it, and then determining what key decisions must be made on the road of parenthood to arrive at self-sufficiency.

Assignment

Start with the end in mind: have a clear vision of what the end result should be.

You can apply the same technique. Picture yourself sitting with your colleagues, all gathered to decide how to improve your company's customer-service image. Starting with the end in mind could mean making a list of words you would like loyal customers to use in describing your sales representatives. Or it could be news headlines you would like *The Wall Street Journal* to publish about your company's superior service.

This clear vision of what you ultimately want to happen is the foundation for good decision-making because it keeps you focused. It keeps a group on track when it starts to veer off course. As the ideas start flying, you'll be in the driver's seat when you ask: How does that help us achieve our vision?

Epilogue

Staying focused on what you want the end to look like not only saves you time, it saves you energy—energy you'll need to reach your ultimate vision.

21

Research Starts With the Ears

Every decision begins with research. What do we know? What do we not know? Let's find out the answers to these questions. We have access to the information, but more often than not, it is with other people. So, our research usually requires listening to others.

But often, we are not good listeners. Listening begins with hearing. We need to do more listening and less talking. One of the greatest problems in customer service is not hearing what the customer is saying. If we do a good job of listening, we learn all kinds of good things. People tell us good, usable information all the time. We just have to listen and pay attention.

> ### *Assignment*
>
> Practice listening. Visit various retail stores and see the difference between good sales clerks and those who don't listen well.

All too often, we want to talk, not listen. When we talk, we learn nothing. And the more we talk, the less likely others will talk to us. You've been there too. You walk into the hardware store and tell the clerk, "I'm working on my deck and…" He interrupts and starts telling you about all the deck materials they have, and where they are, and then begins leading you to the right aisles. Of course, he never lets you finish to tell him that you just need a common drill bit, not decking materials! By the time he learns that, you have already wasted 15 minutes in the store.

So, when researching the problem or opportunity, start with listening to what others have to say, and ask good questions. You'll learn a lot.

Epilogue

Good research begins with good listening skills.

22

How to Listen Effectively

Because listening is so important, how do we do a good job?

First, remember that listening is not hearing. Hearing is the active acquisition and translation of sound waves into meaningful concepts. Hearing is in the ears and then the mind.

Listening is the mental activity of attending to someone else's communication with the goal of gaining understanding. Here are some simple tips:

Assignment

Practice some of these techniques on a regular basis, so you can develop an expertise in good, solid listening skills.

1. Focus on the speaker alone; tune out other stimuli.

2. Actively listen. Pay attention to the communication, and tune out other thoughts and concerns you are having.

3. Remember, if you are talking, you are not listening! Minimize your own speaking.

4. Concentrate on learning from what the other person is saying. The goal is understanding.

5. Suspend your preconceptions about the person, the subject, the circumstances. Try to focus on the topic and the listening experience objectively.

6. Keep emotional reactions under control.

7. Use active physical listening techniques: leaning forward during the conversation, maintaining eye contact, and providing positive feedback like nodding of head.

8. Minimize interruptions. Be patient and allow the speaker to finish his or her thoughts.

9. Suspend judgment. It's about listening and learning, not about arguing.

10. Ask good, relevant, and insightful questions.

Epilogue

Listening is one of the most important tools in your decision-making kit. It lets you learn and discover.

23

Techniques for Asking Questions

Beyond listening, asking good questions that elicit quality answers is also part of the research phase of making a decision. When interviewing key players in your information-gathering phase prior to making a decision, think about asking good questions.

Prepare before any discussion by thinking through what information you want to gather and developing potential questions that will elicit that information. Think about questions in two ways:

Assignment

Set up some scenarios and practice these techniques so you become comfortable with this information-gathering tool.

First, create questions in both a closed-ended response (yes/no) followed by questions that are open ended (allow the interviewee to respond with details). Start with the yes/no question. Once you get that response, you can ask the obvious: why or why not? Allow the respondent plenty of time to answer. Often, the longer the answer, the more details you'll get.

For example: Are our customers returning Product X more often than others? Get yes or no. Then, follow up with more questions: Why do you think they are doing that? What are they telling you when they do return the product? Let your customer service reps talk, and listen closely.

Second, ask questions that follow the journalist's tried-and-true key elements of information: who, what, where, when, why, and how—known as the five W's. Who is doing this? What is the reason? Where are they returning the product? When do the customers seem to return them? How are the products coming back? Why do customers say they are returning the product?

Epilogue

The quality of your decision is greatly dependent on the information you are given.

24

Think—Don't React

Robert Frost once said: "The brain is a wonderful organ; it starts working the moment you get up in the morning and does not stop until you get into the office."

Too often this can be true among managers. You've probably run across at least one of them. Almost like a natural reflex, the brain shuts down and they react automatically. Ironically, many of these individuals are probably sharp, intelligent, and well-intentioned people. But one knee-jerk reaction too many and they begin to lose credibility and influence.

Sadly, their reactions are often the result of fear.

Explosive conflicts in decision making can be the result of fear, and so can avoiding making a decision all together. Fear can lead to poor decisions made without having all the necessary facts. Unchecked, fear can quickly carry you away from your vision.

So what drives fear in decisions? Sometimes it's personal insecurity or pressure from the boss. Or maybe it's just burnout.

But there is a cure for this management disorder;

> ### Assignment
>
> Through time, thinking will set you up to succeed. Reaction, however, will set you up to fail. Choose to think, and you will choose to succeed time and again.

it's called "thinking." Reacting is merely action driven by emotions, rather than rationale. Thinking, however, is the antidote because it is decision making based on analysis—analysis of facts, theories, and input from others who may have "been there, done that." This collection of information is known as a base of knowledge, and all good decisions are made on this basis.

Cool rationale, however, can only come by way of an open mind that is ready to ask questions, listen, and truly understand. It puts action to the side, while the brain gets busy considering all information available. That's why the research step of decision-making is so crucial. Though you can never have all the data, this should not preclude you from having as much as you can gather in a given situation.

Epilogue

Good decisions are built on a solid foundation of knowledge, not the shifting sand of reaction.

25

Think Options!

As you develop an appropriate decision, remember that there is always more than one way to accomplish something. So, think about options—different ways of achieving an outcome. Look at options both from the perspective of what outcome you would like to get, as well as options on how to actually achieve each outcome.

As you examine your data, think about the likely potential outcomes you want from your decision. List those outcomes. There

Assignment

Think back on all the techniques you were taught on what to do personally with decisions in your life. Many require you to list pros and cons. This is a similar technique.

may well be more than one acceptable and possible outcome, so list each.

Then, examine each outcome and list the potential ways to achieve that outcome. Again, there's always more than one way to get to a final destination, so think creatively using your gathered information, and identify all the different ways to each outcome.

Then, of course, you have to choose—or, if you are using a consensus process, the group needs to choose. But they do so by having all the information organized in logical ways.

Epilogue

Armed with information and options, you, or your group, are ready to examine solutions and to make effective decisions.

26

Prioritize—Know What Decisions to Make When

Sometimes you find yourself in a position in which decision making is your primary task. This is not unusual among senior managers and corporate leaders. When this happens, you have multiple decisions to make, many of which you are working on at the same time.

So, there are some fairly simple rules:

First, make those decisions that are needed by others as quickly as you can. Don't skimp on your research or analysis, but be mindful of others' needs.

Second, for those decisions that don't need to be made right away, create a simple time line beginning with the date the decision is needed, and back plan from there.

Third, when you know the situation needs a collaborative decision, create the time line with the other participants in mind, and with their participation.

Finally, if you aren't certain if the decision is yours to make, make it a priority to find out through discussions and investigations. If

> ### Assignment
>
> Reflect on decisions you have been involved with in the past—yours, others, and collaborative decisions. Did anyone plan the process? Did you have enough time?

it's yours, you want the time to make a good decision; if it's collaborative, you want to be certain you plan for others' participation; if it's someone else's decision to make, you want to provide him with enough time to do a good job.

> ### Epilogue
> *Bad decisions often are the result of rushed decisions. Planning for them makes for better end results.*

27

Seek Input From Others—Even When It's Solely Your Decision

Even if you are making the decision alone, without a group consensus, you need input from others. And if you are going for a consensus decision, then you *really* need input from others! And you should solicit that input.

Talk with or interview anyone who may have a stake in the decision or its outcome. This should include, but is not limited to, other managers and decision makers, your boss or bosses, employees, customers, and vendors. In short, anyone who will be affected in any way by the decision.

This accomplishes two important objectives. First, it demonstrates that you are being thorough and inclusive in your investigations, and in your preparation to make the decision. People like to feel

> ## Assignment
>
> Think back on all the decisions that were made without your input, but that had some kind of effect on you. Now you know why it's important to be as inclusive as possible.

as if they have "done their homework" before making a decision. Second, it makes everyone a player in the decision-making process. Even if you are making an autocratic decision, just asking people for their input makes them feel like you know the decision is important enough to them to ask their opinions.

Obviously this takes time, but it is time well spent.

> ### Epilogue
> *Involving people in your research also involves them in the decision.*

28

Decisions to Save Face

Once you have decided that a decision is yours to make, you should remember that you are not the expert in all things. Often, there are others with special expertise and experience who can help you make these decisions. Take advantage of their advice and counsel.

Assignment

Remember the times you have been asked for advice on a decision? That was someone seeking to make a quality, informed decision.

Remember that a decision made with all the information and advice available is always a better decision than one made by someone who just goes off and decides on his or her own.

Yes, it may well be your decision to make. But consulting others better informs you in the process and gives you much more information and background against which to make a good decision. Don't hesitate; ask.

Epilogue

Informed decisions are always more effective than decisions made without counsel.

29

Consult With Mentors, Veterans in Your Field, Company Experts, and Colleagues

So, if you choose to seek others' advice, who should you consult? You probably already know the answer. First, consult with your fellow managers. Many have gone through the experience and can help you by sharing their experiences. In addition, if your decision will have an affect on their work, you would want their opinion anyway.

Consider consulting other experts in the company. They may not be your fellow managers, but they may well have expertise you need. A very good example is your human resources experts on staff, especially if your decision is going to affect employees in any way. They have seen lots of problems caused by management decisions and can suggest possible effective approaches from real experience.

Consider talking with other veterans in your particular field. You know them from your participation in trade and professional associations. They may have had a similar experience and can share that with you.

Also always consult

> ### *Assignment*
>
> Make an informal list of people you could use as consultants when you are called upon to make an important decision. Use the list as needed.

with your mentor. You have one, right? Your mentor is someone you consult with about your career on a regular basis. Use them to help guide your decision making as well.

> ### Epilogue
> *You know people who can be of help. Use them. Consult with them. They will help you with information and advice. And you'll make a better decision as a result.*

30

Value Others' Insight

All of these other people you are consulting are more than just information providers. Don't consult with people just to say you did so, and then just do what you want. If you do that they will not help you the next time you ask.

Value what they can offer you. Apply their information and recommendations in your thinking processes as you analyze the situation and create a solution (the decision). All too often, people take the approach that they are expected to ask others advice, but then they don't have to take it and can do what the want.

This will almost always lead to two results: first, a poor, personally motivated decision that often backfires.

> ## Assignment
>
> You've been here before. Remember the last time someone asked you for advice and then clearly disregarded it. Will you help them again?

Second, a loss of personal credibility as those who were consulted realize their advice was solicited, but ignored.

When you do consult, make certain you not only use the information and recommendations, but that you tell those you consult that you will do so, and you appreciate their help.

> ### Epilogue
> *The information and advice you get from others is truly valuable.*

31

Have a Brainstorm

You've probably done this before: a brainstorm exercise. It can be done individually or with a group (a group is usually best).

You set a task or ask a question and everyone participating thinks of things appropriate to that subject. The only rules in brainstorming are that there are no rules. Okay, maybe a few. Set a time limit for ideas and always have some mechanism to record what you (or all the participants) come up with. Other than that, anything goes. No idea is too small, no idea is inappropriate.

Assignment

Since most of us have participated in brainstorming sessions, remember your participation in one. Remember how some really unique ideas came up that you might not have thought of alone.

This process provides you with lots of really good ideas—ideas that you would not have thought about otherwise. In group settings, people feed off of others ideas to come up with ideas they would never have thought of alone.

The result: You get a list of lots of ideas pertaining to your problem, your task, or your opportunity. Some will not be valuable, and some will not be practical. But some will be new ideas you would never have thought of to bring to the decision process.

Epilogue

Groups often provide more high-quality ideas and solutions than individuals. That's why we do so much group work.

32

Weighing Pros and Cons

Okay, you've probably done this before: You get out a piece of paper. At the top you write two words creating two columns: pro and con. You state your solution (the decision). Then you simply think through that decision listing all of the positive results of the decision under pros, and all of the potentially negative results under cons.

Assignment

Try this with the next decision you have to make, either professionally or personally.

Result: You have a clear list of advantages and disadvantages for that decision. Now do it for every possible decision you can make to provide a solution to a problem or take advantage of an opportunity. Each one results in a list of advantages and disadvantages.

Use the lists to weigh the potential decisions.

Epilogue

Yes, this is a very old technique and probably should not be used alone. But it is still valuable, and is often a good starting point for any decision.

33

There Are No Mistakes, Only Lessons

Have you ever made a mistake? Come on, fess up! We have all made some mistakes in our lives. Some personal, some professional; making mistakes is simply part of life. We don't let the possibility of making a mistake keep us from making decisions or getting our work done, do we?

So, don't be afraid of making a mistake when you have to make a decision. If it goes wrong or your solution turns out badly, use it as a learning tool, not only for yourself but for everyone involved. Then fix it and move on.

Assignment

Think back on any manager you have known in the past who simply could not make a decision because he was afraid it would be the wrong decision. Remember the problems the lack of a decision cost?

Mistakes are part of life and can often be repaired, so don't let that possibility keep you from making decisions.

Epilogue

Don't let the fear of failure stop you from being the effective manager you can be.

34

Risk Is Good—Embrace It!

There is always a level of risk in every decision. After all, if the decision were 100 percent clear, we wouldn't need people to make decisions; we would let computers make them. But we don't, do we? Because there are lots of intangibles that have to be considered.

Risk is part of the process of decision making. What is the risk? On the one hand, we risk failure. We risk not achieving the goal or objective because we make a bad decision or the wrong decision. We risk someone else's job. We risk our job!

> ### Assignment
>
> Examine your own willingness to take risks. They come with the territory, so start realizing that you will have to take a risk with every decision you make.

On the other hand, we also risk success. We risk over achieving on any goal or objective. We risk having everyone involved look good as a result of the decision. We risk our own success in our jobs.

As managers, part of our job is to make decisions. Every decision implies risk, so live with it and move on. Make the decision, and be prepared to work with the results.

Epilogue

The greatest risk you can take is not making the decision and risking success—for you and for your organization.

35

Leverage Risk for a Calculated Outcome

Okay, we know we have to take risks with every decision, but we don't just throw ourselves to the fates, do we? Of course not. We have to calculate the risk for each potential decision and weigh the potential outcomes.

Remember that pros and cons exercise? It can help you identify which decision will provide the likeliest positive outcome. Remember those recommendations from others? They can help you weigh the decision possibilities so that you can try to achieve the best possible outcome.

Assignment

In decision-making situations, some outcomes will require higher risks. Can you remember decisions you observed or participated in that were like that? How did they turn out? What can you learn from those experiences or observations?

That's the task. Calculating the likely outcomes of each decision to determine which decision option will result in the best outcome—for your organization, for your people, and for you.

But sometimes the greater outcomes also require taking the higher risks. You could, perhaps, take a lesser risk, but you'll also achieve a lesser outcome. You have to weigh the options and determine how much risk is acceptable for the measured outcome you are likely to get from each option.

Epilogue
In almost all cases, higher risk will lead to greater rewards (outcomes). You have to decide which level is appropriate for you.

36

Avoid Making Decisions From Ego

We always want to make good decisions for good reasons. That will accomplish good things for our organization and our people.

So avoid the potential for making a decision because it's "good for me." Or making a decision because you have the power. Ego is a terrible thing to allow into your decision-making process. It almost always turns out badly—for you and for the organization.

Make your decisions based on good information, good recommendations, and thoughtful analysis focused on achieving the best outcomes for everyone. Remember that ego focuses on yourself. Good decision makers focus on the organization and others.

Assignment

Reflect on decisions you have seen made by managers who did so because "they could" or because it was good for them. How did these decisions turn out?

Epilogue
Ego should be left out of the decision-making process.

37

Avoid Making Decisions Political

Every organization has internal politics. To deny that would be foolish. Yet, using political motivations to make decisions often turns out badly as well. Politics usually implies conflict between various groups in an organization or a community. Political motivations are always recognizable. The information is different from what you have gathered from other objective sources; recommendations are not consistent with the organization's overall objective, and would not serve one group more than another without any significant gain to the organization.

Allowing these inputs into your process can result in biased decision making. These decisions tend not to be as good as they could be, and, worse, are often recognized by others who are just as biased, which damages your credibility.

> ### *Assignment*
>
> Remember decisions you have seen made by others that were politically biased. How did they turn out? How did it turn out for the decision maker?

Thus, allowing politics to play a role in your decision-making process is allowing one faction to gain advantage over another, and not necessarily for good or right reasons. So avoid political reasons and arguments in your decision making if you can. Again, focus on the greatest gain for the greatest number.

As a side note, of course, we can't always avoid politics. Sometimes people will attempt to influence you in your decision making not based on rational information or an honest focus on a positive outcome, but on personal gain or political (organizational) gain. When this happens, recognize it, acknowledge it, and weigh it carefully before allowing that influence to have too much weight in your end result.

Epilogue

Politics are often unsavory, and especially unsavory inside organizations. Avoid allowing political motivations to play a role in your decision making.

38

Avoid the Proverbial Knee-Jerk Reaction

"They did what?! Even after I told them not to?! Well, I'll just teach them a thing or two!"

Hold on just a doggone minute. You are having a knee-jerk reaction. Somebody has done something you told them specifically not to do. And now it's come to your attention. Your immediate reaction is to take them to task for it. But...

You are reacting from emotions and with insufficient information. Knee-jerk reactions are common and understandable, but should always be avoided. Emotion

Assignment

You've seen these before. Remember what they are like.

is rarely a good element in decision making. Never make a decision when you are mad at someone. Never make a decision when you are overly happy with someone. Wait and allow the emotion to pass and then gather information and analyze it.

We rarely have all the information we need in these circumstances, either. If we allow our emotions to rule, we forget that the first step in the decision-making process is to gather information. But if you allow yourself a knee-jerk reaction, you operate only with the initial information that caused that reaction. There's always more information available than we have initially.

In our previous example, investigate first. You may well discover that there was a very good reason someone violated your guidance. They may even deserve a commendation, not a hollering.

Epilogue

Recognize your knee-jerk emotional reactions for what they are and calm down first before taking action.

39

Avoid Group Think

Group think is a phenomenon in group consensus situations in which the group avoids conflict. In doing so, it fails to properly question information, to critically analyze data and potential alternatives, and to reach decisions without vital discussion.

Groups that are too homogeneous (too much alike) often result in group think.

The problem, of course, is that group think is dishonest. Oh, not intentionally. These groups don't set out to engage in group think. It just happens because everyone is so in tune with each other that they don't question any of the information they are gathering. They don't effectively analyze alternative solutions; rather, they gravitate to one alternative because it "seems" right. Then they justify that outcome without really examining the others.

Assignment

Watch group think happening around you, in meetings you attend and in ad hoc or regular work groups you participate in regularly.

How can you tell if your group is engaging in group think? The first indicator is that there are no alternative information sources from outside the group. Second, there is little argument or conflict. Everyone just agrees with everyone else. No disagreement. No debate. No factions aligned to promote one solution on another.

When this happens, your group is engaged in group think, and any decision it makes is likely to be a poor one at best.

Epilogue

Recognize group think and avoid it. Restructure the group if necessary.

40

Group Think Is Manipulation— It's Not Consensus

The truth is that overly homogeneous groups that engage in group think, even unknowingly, are manipulating the decision process to their advantage. They are so alike in their thinking that they ignore other facts that may disagree with their facts, ignore other alternatives that may not be as advantageous to them as their option, and make decisions that tend to benefit them as a group.

As a result, they have not only hijacked the decision-making process, they have also manipulated the decision in their favor and possibly to the detriment of the organization, or at least other groups in the organization.

This is really dishonest decision making and absolutely must be avoided. History is replete with examples of group think. The decline of IBM Corporation in the early 1980s is a great example. These employees and executives thought alike, worked alike, even dressed alike. They got trapped in group think.

> ### Assignment
>
> You've probably seen group think in action. Identify one decision that resulted from group think and remember how it turned out.

Epilogue

Practice consensus decision making and avoid group think.

41

Remember the Organizational "Layers" Involved

In making the decision on whom to involve, remember that it will depend greatly on where in the organization the outcomes will be felt. Generally speaking, there are three "layers" of any organization.

The first is at the lowest level, with the immediate supervisor of a group of people. Decisions here usually only involve those people and their work processes, so these decisions rarely involve others outside this small group.

The second layer includes decisions that involve more than one group and perhaps people in multiple departments and even locations. These decisions require more coordination, research, consultation, and even participation.

The third layer involves the organization as a whole—everyone in it and every process. These are complex decisions that will ultimately involve all key managers and the senior leadership team of the organization.

Who should be involved in a decision can often depend on the layer it affects.

Epilogue

Understanding the layers means knowing who needs to be involved.

42

Whoa! You're Challenging the Status Quo?

This is one of the major barriers to decision making; people are resistant to change.

This isn't rocket science. We all know people are uncomfortable with change. Every research project discovers this. Recognize that if your decision has the potential to make significant change in the organization, or for some of its people, you are going to get resistance, not just to the decision implementation, but also to the decision itself.

People are comfortable with the status quo. They like how things are going now. They are afraid of change. Change means uncertainty. Change means new and/or different. Change is a challenge to their current status.

Recognize that as you investigate and create alternative solutions in preparation for making a decision, if the status quo is potentially threatened, people in the organization will be resistant. Sometimes they are resistant enough to provide bad or biased information., perhaps resistant enough to provide biased recommendations and opinions.

Assignment

Learn to recognize resistance that results from a challenge to the status quo. Double-check information; gather lots of opinion and recommendations from a wide variety of people; weigh the information and recommendations carefully.

Recognize the behaviors of resistance and weigh that as you evaluate your input and make your decision. Then, recognize that you will have barriers to overcome as you "sell" your decision and get it implemented inside the organization.

Epilogue
People don't like change, so they will not necessarily help you make changes.

43

When Culture Stands in the Way

Organizations all have a "culture." Culture is their set of rules and behavior expectations, their processes for making things happen, and their expectations for how people will behave and how the organization behaves. These are cultural norms.

Unfortunately, sometimes this culture can be a barrier to good decision making in the same way that challenging the status quo can be. An organizational culture may dictate one set of behaviors that your decision might violate. It might suggest that boundaries between union and management are inviolate and you can't consult with employees on a decision because they are union. It might have a rigid hierarchy of management that bars you from talking with senior managers about your decision.

These kinds of organizational culture norms can sometimes prevent you from doing a good job at decision making because they bar you from access to key information or key people.

When this happens, the best strategy is to acknowledge the cultural norm and work around it as best you can. For example, if your hierarchical organization's norms suggest that a manager doesn't have access to a vice president, then work through someone else to approach the vice president with the questions you need answered. If you can't directly address

Assignment

Examine your own organization. What are its cultural norms? Are any of them potential barriers to good decision making? How would you get around those barriers?

some employees for any reason, find someone who can act as your surrogate. If you don't normally have access to certain information in the organization, either ask for permission to access it and justify your need, or find someone who does have that access and recruit him or her to obtain the information for you.

Epilogue

While cultural norms in organizations can be significant barriers to good decision making, with effort, these barriers can be overcome without upsetting the apple cart.

44

Ambiguity—Applying the Law of Co-orientation

Ambiguity is the state of not knowing everything you need to understand something. As we investigate to determine what information is important for us to have in making our decision, we are in a state of ambiguity because we don't know everything we need to know yet. Thus, we investigate.

In group consensus processes, the members of the group must have a tolerance for this ambiguity while the group investigates.

Assignment

Your task in calling any group together to make a consensus agreement is to ensure that the information discovered is shared with everyone in the group as it comes to its agreement.

Moreover, the investigators must provide their information to everyone in the group. That is co-orientation, a situation in which everyone in the group is armed with the same information everyone else has.

This leads to a co-orientation consensus. This means the group not only has all the accurate information, but has reached agreement on the decision or solution. Your task, as the group facilitator or leader who brought the group together, is to ensure that everyone shares all their information so co-orientation is achieved.

Epilogue

Accuracy and completeness of information plus agreement leads to co-orientation.

45

Look for the Win-Win Result

Rarely does a winner-take-all mentality win friends and influence people. To get others to buy into a decision, think "mutually beneficial."

Leaders in industries such as government, pharmaceuticals, land development, and utilities often find themselves trying to reach consensus decisions with groups that can range from the adversarial to the downright hostile. Those who are successful in partnering with community and activist groups have learned to find the win-win, the decision that provides an equally beneficial result to all parties involved.

This win-win approach can be applied also to interdepartmental decisions. After all, internal decisions are likely to involve

Assignment

Start with understanding the agenda, needs, and sensitivities of the other parties at the table. There is no better starting place for a win-win decision than knowing where people are coming from. The more you can learn about the intentions and needs of others involved, the more likely you are to walk away with a win-win in your pocket—and people's respect to boot.

people from different divisions and departments with slightly varying agendas, needs, and sensitivities.

But you can't come to a win-win result flying by the seat of your pants. It takes forethought, honesty, transparency, patience, and reasonable expectations. It also takes compromise—a willingness to give in order to get.

But how do you get there? Again, the magic bullet can be found in doing your homework.

Epilogue

Transform a winner-takes-all mentality into a win-win solution that makes all parties happy.

46

Decisions That Require a Strategy

So, there is the simple, and there is the complex. When it comes to decisions, they run the gamut. And some decisions require you to get creative and pull out all the stops. That's right—you'll have to develop a strategic plan. That means you have to make decisions about decisions, and possibly even make decisions within decisions.

Is your head spinning yet? As you've probably guessed, decisions that require a strategy are usually among the complex. For example, corporations make decisions all the time on how they'll influence government or consumer decisions.

Think about it. Just about every decision we make is about influencing someone else's decision, whether that is to vote a certain way, buy a specific brand, join a particular group, or take a given action. And the higher the stakes, the more strategic thinking you'll have to muster.

In fact, the whole concept of win-win is about

Assignment

Do some digging for information that shines light on the situation, the players involved, and what each party wants to get out of the decision. Then develop your action plan: think about what direction you'll take, what tactics you'll need to influence the situation or project, who you'll need to have in your court, and the time line to move forward with implementing your plan. Then last, but never, never least, is a plan for how you'll evaluate the results of your decision.

developing a strategy before you ever get to the decision-making table. You could call it a road map, helping you maneuver through the interpersonal nuances that can stymie group decision making, and delay critical decisions from getting off the ground.

So what goes into developing a strategic plan? Research, analysis, and evaluation. Wow! Sounds like a lot of work, doesn't it? It is, but mustering this kind of thinking is powerful in coming to educated and well-planned decisions. And this type of planning differentiates the wheat from the chaff in decision making.

Epilogue

When the decision goes beyond the simple, muster your creative thinking skills and pull out the big gun in your decision-making arsenal: strategic planning.

47

The Law of Diminishing Returns

We have all experienced this before, so we know it's true even without all the studies that have demonstrated its veracity. There comes a point in group discussions (or even in an individual investigation) where little more will be learned, and what is learned will not be significant. Another point will be reached when the group discussion has come around to the same issues for a second or third time. Nothing new will emerge and there will be little to show for additional discussion.

The group, or its leader (probably you), will need to recognize when this point of

Assignment

You have been in groups that reach this point of diminishing returns before. Remember what happened then? How inefficient and time wasting it was?

diminishing returns has been reached and move from discussion to decision making. To continue will be to waste people's time and achieve almost nothing. And it delays the decision.

This point is almost always reached when 90 percent of the information needed to make a decision is known, and all of the alternatives and their arguments have been determined and discussed at least twice. After this point, the group will flounder around and accomplish little.

At this point, the group and/or its leader must move to the decision and focus on obtaining that decision. Some techniques include setting a time at which point the decision must be made; establishing a voting schedule, or even creating an advocate for each alternative and have them present and debate among themselves for the rest of the group.

Epilogue

Remember that once the point of diminishing returns has been reached, the group's effectiveness is significantly reduced. It's time to make the decision.

48

Banishing the "What Ifs"

"Yes, but what if…?"

How many times have you heard that? You are in a decision-making group and a few people keep coming up with the what ifs. And they can keep coming up with new ones forever. The group, or its leader, needs to recognize that some important what ifs are necessary for alternative development. But to deal with every little "what if" is a barrier to consensus and decision making.

All too often, group members will come up with

Assignment

As you recognize these extraneous "what ifs" beginning to surface in group discussion, move to stop them before they cause problems.

completely irrelevant "what ifs"—like, "What if Johnny doesn't like the solution?" Unless Johnny is the president of the company, his concerns are probably not relevant to the decision. So don't let these keep coming up. They'll keep you from getting to the decision.

Create a mechanism to identify each important alternative—each important "what if" and then banish the rest from the group discussion. Convince the group that those alternative situations have all been addressed and others are simply not relevant.

Epilogue

Constant "what ifs" will keep the group distracted and off course to a good, viable decision.

49

Keep an Open Mind

As you investigate, gather information, create alternatives, analyze those alternatives, and come to a decision, keep an open mind to possibilities you may not have considered before you started the process.

Avoid allowing preconceived notions about how to solve a problem or what is best for the organization to color your research and your analysis—and ultimately your judgment and decision. Be open to new ideas. Be open to new factors you might not have considered.

Assignment

Be open-minded about information and alternatives. Remember that you are looking for the best, not the most appropriate, decision.

For new factors, look for such things as you examine the problem, challenge, or opportunity.

The reason you use this process is to get the best information and the finest recommendations available. In doing so, be open to new ideas, new thinking, and new approaches you yourself may not have considered. In group consensus decision making, remember that everyone's ideas are valid, and that there may well be good ideas lurking in the most unusual of places. Be open to those.

Epilogue

Good ideas sometimes live in unusual places. Look for them.

50

Let Go of Assumptions

We all have assumptions about lots of things. Truthfully, we can't effectively operate without assumptions.

However, in decision-making processes, we want to let go of all of our assumptions—especially any that have any bearing on the decision we need to make. If it is a group consensus effort, everyone in the group needs to let go of their assumptions.

Assignment

Identify your assumptions about the organization, its people, its goals and objectives, and everything else, and open yourself to new information. Make new assumptions during the decision-making process—don't rely on old ones.

71

Assumptions are the things we simply take for granted as truths. We simply accept them without questioning them. Usually, we're right. Usually, our assumptions are based on knowledge and personal experience, and they are valid.

But when making important decisions, we need to let those assumptions go and assume nothing. In fact, we should even question any assumption that comes up and determine its validity. Don't ever assume anything is true until you have validated its truthfulness.

After all, making a decision based on a faulty assumption leads to a faulty decision.

Epilogue

Remember what "assume" spells. Assumptions can make an "a__" of "u" and "me."

51

Let Go of Fear

Fear is the mind killer. Fear of decision making, fear of a particular decision, fear of taking a risk, fear of involving others, fear of not making a good decision. Fear can be a terrible barrier to good decision making.

When it comes time to make a decision, you must let go of any fears you have. The organization and its people are depending upon you to make a good decision, but fear of that decision will impair your ability to do so.

Fear of the decision can easily cause you to make a bad decision. Fear of the outcome of a decision can easily lead you to make the wrong decision, because you are afraid of the consequences of your decision.

Fear kills thinking processes, taints information with inappropriate values, precludes you from consid-

Assignment

When faced with a decision-making situation, the first thing you must do is banish fear from the process.

ering potential solutions, and keeps you from doing a good job at the process of making a decision.

Epilogue
Fear is the decision killer. Don't let it in.

52

See the Possibilities

After gathering information about the situation, challenge, or opportunity, your next task is to create some potential alternative solutions (the decision). In doing so, be open and receptive to many different possibilities.

Look for the new and the innovative. Look for the creative approaches that may lead to enhanced outcomes. Be open to different ideas and different approaches than have been used in the past.

Then analyze them all to determine which solution is the right solution. In doing so, again, be open to fresh approaches and creative solutions that might lead to outcomes.

But remember, too, that your decision will lead to outcomes, which lead to results. So visualize as much as possible those potential outcomes for each of your possible solutions. This visualization will help you choose which solution is the right decision.

> ### Assignment
>
> Be open to the new and creative. The fresh ideas. But remember to be focused on outcomes and results.

> ### Epilogue
> *History has demonstrated time and again that fresh ideas and creative solutions often result in outcomes well beyond those originally intended.*

53

Don't Be Afraid of Conflict

As in any organization, when decisions have to be made, there is a high likelihood of conflict, both during the decision-making process and after. However, this likelihood of conflict cannot be a barrier to decision making.

In fact, some conflict is healthy for the decision-making process itself. If you are making the decision alone, getting conflicting opinions and

> ### Assignment
>
> Recall decisions that involved organizational or personal conflict. Note those that were used and controlled to provide healthy discussion to the process and those that were allowed to get personal and become detrimental to the process.

recommendations provides you with alternatives and different thinking. That's useful. If this decision will be a group consensus process, then conflict within the group is a good thing as well, so long as it is controlled and focused on the decision and not the personal relationships. Again, conflict (disagreement) should be perceived as healthy and not negative.

Don't fear conflict; encourage it and control it to help you make the decision or allow the group to make a good decision.

Epilogue

Anticipate conflict during decision making and use it to enhance, not detract from, the process.

54

Change Is a Natural Catalyst for Conflict

Almost every decision will require change in some way. And change is the natural catalyst for conflict in organizations. So expect change and expect conflict.

Now we have to discuss the nature of change. As you present change to your group, your employees, or your organization, note that change—while not always good—is usually a healthy process for all organizations. After all, if Thomas Edison had not continually changed the various filaments in his light bulbs (even after his assistants suggested he was

Assignment

Review changes in organizations you have been a part of in the past. What has been the effect? How was it handled?

wasting his time), we may not have electric incandescent lights today.

So keep in mind that change is usually good, but often traumatic, for organization's and the people within them. As a result, change generates conflict. The key is to anticipate that conflict and manage it positively. Use the conflict to inform your decision making.

Epilogue

Decisions almost always mean change, and change leads to conflict. Manage it.

55

Change Is the Fuel of Progress

Progress in almost every endeavor and field has come from changes. Changes lead to progress. Lack of change leads to near-certain death for companies and organizations. So change is almost always a positive.

Today almost everyone who wears a watch has a digital, quartz movement. No main springs and fewer mechanisms have led to a more reliable and accurate timepiece. Do you know who invented the quartz movement

---

Assignment

Review changes in other businesses you are familiar with and see what happened to their organizations as a result of those changes.

---

watch? The Swiss! Yes, the makers of fine watches invented the quartz movement watch. But when the managers of the watch company saw a watch without a mainspring, they rejected it as unnecessary. But they still showed it around at trade shows.

Folks at Timex saw this new kind of watch and changed the industry forever. In just a few decades, the Swiss went from owning more than 85 percent of the market in watches to losing most of that business to Timex and new upstarts. Today, Swiss watchmakers have only about 10 percent of the watch market.

The Swiss saw a change and rejected it. Timex else saw that same change and history was made. So embrace change.

Epilogue

Change leads to growth. Lack of change leads to stagnation and death.

56

Don't Take It Personally

As you explore information and options in any decision-making situation, remember that you want people to give you their honest and accurate information and recommendations. So when they tell you something you don't really want to hear, or say that an idea is dumb, remember that they are reacting to the idea or the information—not you.

Don't take these comments personally. They are not attacks on you. They are not criticisms of you personally. They are just other people's honest assessments of the situation or the idea.

Assignment

Remember when someone you know took something personally when all you were doing was giving them your honest opinion about an idea or a solution?

If you take these things personally, you risk damaging the decision-making process and you certainly risk damaging your relationships with the people you are asking.

It ain't about you, it's about the solution.

Epilogue

Remain objective about the decision and the process. Don't take things personally.

57

Don't Make It Personal

On the other hand, don't make it personal when you ask people for their input. If you do, you are setting yourself up for failure. Each decision you are called upon to make should be made impartially and without your personal stake invested in the outcome.

If you make it personal, others will notice, and will not give you honest information, opinions, or feedback. They,

Assignment

Do you remember when a colleague took something you said too personally? Did you mean it that way? Probably not. Remember this circumstance and let it be your guide.

too, are conscious of the relationship they maintain with you, and will be unwilling to damage that relationship by saying something you will react to negatively or reject.

If you allow this to happen, you will not get good information or recommendations, and your decision is likely to be flawed as a result. Then you really will suffer from the decision.

Epilogue

Stay objective. The decision is not about you; it's about the best solution for the organization.

58

Handling Those Who Disagree

If conflict is inevitable, then how do you handle those who disagree? Remember we acknowledge that it's not personal—for them or for us, so disagreement may well be a positive.

At some point, disagreement should change to acceptance. Total agreement is not required, even in a consensus situation. Remember that consensus requires only that the group accept the decision as a whole.

In handling those who disagree, make certain you do a few key things:

- ◆ Make certain their voices have been heard—that you have given them an opportunity to present their positions.

- ◆ Make certain that you (or the group) have engaged with them via questions and discussion, so they believe they had a fair hearing.

79

♦ Make certain all of
   their questions and
   concerns have been
   addressed.

♦ Remember that
   they need to accept
   the decision, not
   necessarily agree with it.

Assignment

Practice listening and discussion techniques to handle those who disagree.

A final note: Do not change you mind just because you want to avoid conflict with someone else.

Epilogue

In most cases, if handled correctly, acceptance often morphs into agreement through time if the decision returns a positive result.

59

Base Your Decision on the Merits of the Proposal or Solution

While we have discussed this item before, let's be clear: the decision must be based on the facts in the case and the merits of the solution. It must be the best solution for the greatest number.

This requires that you (or your group) be objective in evaluating information and courses of action.

This requires that you be thorough in your investigations and thorough in you analysis of the potential outcomes of each alternative.

> ### Assignment
>
> Review the materials we have discussed to ensure you understand the value of objectivity.

This requires that you weigh in the balance all alternatives and select the best one based on its merits—not emotion, not politics, not personal preferences, not for the advantage of any individual group.

> ### Epilogue
>
> *You are attempting to reach the best solution, not the acceptable solution.*

60

Resist the Urge to Go With the First Option on the Table

Sometimes we discover a solution that will clearly work early in our investigations. Groups do this as well. Then the inclination is to cry victory, select that solution, and move on.

While the solution (decision) might well be acceptable, it's certainly not the best decision because you have not yet developed nor reviewed any other possibilities. Selecting the first option that seems to solve the problem denies the opportunity to discover that there might be other options out there that would solve the problem even better.

> ### Assignment
>
> Constantly remind yourself that there is always more than one way to solve any problem.

It's human nature to discover a fix and then implement

it to come to a quick decision that will clearly work and settle on that decision. But you must resist that temptation. That solution might be right, but there might be much better options out there just waiting to be discovered. Take the time to make the right decision, not the easy decision.

Epilogue

The goal is to make the <u>best</u> decision, not the quickest decision.

61

Resist the Urge to Go With Very Limited Facts

As you enter into you research and investigation phase of decision making, you start discovering information and facts. Sometimes these can be very solid and compelling facts that come to light early in the process. Other times, we think we have very quickly discovered the key information and want to move right to a decision based on this preliminary and important data.

But wait; don't rush this process. Never presume that, just because you have some really key and important information early in your decision-making pro-

Assignment

Remind yourself that every decision is important to someone, and every decision should be researched thoroughly and well.

cess that suggests the right decision, there is not a valuable a set of facts out there yet to be discovered.

Don't presume that because you came up with two very good solutions early in the process that there is not a better solution yet to be discovered.

Don't shortcut this process. Follow it through. Research and investigate thoroughly. Talk to everyone who should be involved—everyone. Then decide.

Epilogue

Never shortcut the process. Look for every solution, not just the quick and easy ones.

62

Resist the Urge to Dismiss Problems That Require Dynamic Levels of Decisions

Some problems seem to require multiple levels of decision—perhaps one that you can make and then two that your boss has to make, and yet another that a group or team needs to make. Sometimes these levels can seem daunting and almost insurmountable.

They are not; they are just difficult. But they can be navigated with some careful planning.

Assignment

Review other such multilevel decisions you have experienced throughout the years. How were they handled?

The easiest way to handle these kinds of multiple decisions at different levels is to create an ad hoc team with the key decision makers involved. Create a single process that examines the problem from all levels, explores the solutions at each

83

level, and discusses the possible solutions and how they interact with each other.

This process is more difficult and more time consuming. But don't avoid it just because it seems too tough to handle.

Epilogue
Never avoid a decision that has to be made, no matter how complex or difficult. They only get more complex and difficult over time.

63

Do What's Right!

Moviemaker Spike Lee made a film early in his career called *Do the Right Thing*, which was greeted with high acclaim.

In decision making, we always have to keep in mind that doing the right thing is our goal. We need to do it for everyone involved. We need to make the best decision that can be made. That decision needs to effectively and efficiently solve the problem, meet the challenge, or take advantage of the opportunity.

It needs to benefit as many people as possible and harm as few as possible.

Assignment
Review your ethics and responsibilities. Remember them when it comes time to make decisions.

And it needs to be accomplished in a reasonable and practical time frame.

When we make decisions, we must "do the right thing."

Epilogue

Remember that as decision makers we have responsibilities to everyone else involved in the process. It's important to get it right.

64

Walking With Integrity

We seem to talk about integrity a lot these days. But there's probably a reason for that: a lack of integrity at too many levels by too many people.

So what is integrity? Wikipedia describes it as: "the basing of one's actions on a consistent framework of principles."

Decisions must be made based on your personal and professional framework of guiding principles for life behavior, such as your personal ethics, and your professional standards of behavior. If you believe that everyone should be treated equally, then that principle should infuse every decision you make.

Assignment

Make sure you have a clear understanding of your personal life principles.

Epilogue

Integrity is expected and, once lost, is difficult to regain. Behave according to your professional standards and you'll be well on your way to good decision making.

65

No Decision Is *a Decision*

All too often you've seen this. A manager has a decision to make but fails to make it. He delays it indefinitely, or puts it off because she is not ready, doesn't have enough information, and hasn't evaluated all the potential solutions and alternatives. And the decision never gets made.

We need to remember that this lack of a decision is a decision. And it's a bad decision. It clearly communicates to everyone involved that the issue is not sufficiently important to this manager for him or her to actually get a decision made. Others will see that as a decision.

And it will damage the organization, the manager's credibility, and the morale of the people involved.

Yes, there are exceptions. Sometimes not making a decision is an intentional decision to allow the situation to continue. If you are going to do that, communicate it that way. Don't just let it sit and fester.

> ### Assignment
>
> You probably remember a situation when a manager simply failed to make a decision that needed to be made. It ended badly, didn't it?

Epilogue

Don't leave decisions unmade unless it is intentional, and exceptional.

66

Don't Be a Buridan's Ass

This is a decision-making technique you can use when two alternative courses of action appear to be equally attractive or positive and you need to decide between the two. This technique suggests that if the positives are equal, focus on the negatives.

To use this method, list all the negative points or drawbacks to each alternative. The one with the fewest negatives is probably the best solution.

You see, when we find two solutions of equal benefit, we often lose sight of the negatives. This method forces us to focus on the whole decision, negatives included.

So where did Buridan's Ass come from? It's an old fable that places an ass between two equally large bales of hay. The ass can't decide which bale to turn and eat from because they are both so attractive. Because of its indecision, the ass starves to death in front of a wealth of hay.

Assignment

Recall the tale of Buridan's Ass. It will remind you when you need to use this method.

Epilogue

Sometimes focusing on the negatives lets us eliminate one of two equally good-looking alternatives.

67

Take a Step Backward to Review

Somewhere during the process of decision making, we often get overwhelmed. There is a lot of information, and we get lots of recommendations. We've had lots of group meetings with lots of discussion, and sometimes we just feel like the problem will overwhelm us.

This often happens because we become so immersed in the decision-making process that we lose sight of the goal. We get numbed by the facts, information, statistics, recommendations, discussions, and so on.

> ### *Assignment*
>
> Remember to conduct a personal review when you get too close to the issue; keep your mentors handy to help.

When this happens, step back and take a break. Review everything you have done. Review all your information. Visit with a mentor and discuss what you have learned. Sometimes a solid review of everything you have learned and a discussion with an impartial outside mentor can help bring clarity to the decision.

Epilogue

A general review of all your information is often the final step in making the decision.

68

Sometimes You Need to Use Brakes

There are some decisions that seem rushed, and that's because they are.

We need to keep in mind that not every decision needs to be made today, or even tomorrow.

Yet, sometimes the process gets moving so quickly and with such energy that is seems to get away from us. When that happens, we risk a bad decision simply because it is rushed.

If you see this happening, hit the brakes—hard! Stop the process, even for a short period of time, to review the process and the status. Evaluate again the time frame this decision needs to be made within. If there is more time, then you can slow down the process. If there is not more time, then you can reorganize the process to allow you to better control it, so you get everything done without it getting away from you.

Assignment

Keep an eye on the process to make certain it's not getting out of control.

If it does get away from you and a decision gets made without proper due process, then it's likely you'll have other decisions to make down the road—decisions on how to fix the consequences of this decision!

Epilogue
A rushed, uncontrolled, and uncoordinated decision equals of a bad decision.

69

Comparing Outcomes With Goals and Objectives

Okay, so you're ready to face the music of your decision. Where do you begin?

Start with a trip down memory lane: What goals and objectives did you set as a result of your decisions? How were you going to measure success?

If you made these determinations upfront, as part of your strategic-planning process, you will have a turnkey measurement to determine if your outcomes were aligned with what you set out to do in the first place.

Assignment

Compare the results of your decisions to your original goals and objectives to determine if your decision created the outcomes you originally planned.

to determine if your outcomes were aligned with what you set out to do in the first place.

Be careful of mistaking outcomes with outputs. The latter is easy to measure, such as how many units of new product you pushed into the market. But an outcome is how much revenue you recouped from product sales.

According to Dr. Robert Kaplan and Dr. David Norton, founders of the Balanced Scorecard theory, this tendency to measure what's easy is a weakness in many organizations. As a result, they tend to measure output, such as how many product units were pushed into the market in a given time frame. But remember, the outcome is the result of the outputs.

Epilogue

The goals and objectives that originally guided your decision are the litmus factors for truly evaluating success or failure.

70

Overcoming Mental Decision Blocks

You can become mentally fatigued when making decisions, and that can lead to mental blocks that stifle your thinking and leave you feeling frustrated.

But there are a number of techniques you can use to overcome mental blocks. Most of those techniques encourage you to rest or have fun. Yes, that's right! If you're feeling mentally fatigued or just fresh out of ideas, stop! Step away from the decision-making table—now!

If you're mentally fatigued, you've overdone it. To overcome the block, you need a change of scenery, activity, perspective, or just some good old-fashioned rest and relaxation. By shifting the brain's focus, you use the different parts of your brain. For instance, if you've been crunching numbers to come to a critical financial decision, you've been

Assignment

Read on for a number of techniques that help you tap into your internal tag team. Try one, try two, or try them all. But learn what options you have when you've pushed your mind to the limit.

using the left side of your brain. And if you've developed a block you just can't push through, that's your left side yelling "uncle!"

You may need to step away from the decision for awhile and give the right side of your brain a workout, get a different set of juices pumping. Think about parenting for a moment. Parenting is always easier when there are two. When the kids wear one parent down, the other can step in and take over, bringing fresh energy, ideas, and strategies to the situation. Your brain is like dual parenting—two sides that can work as a tag team.

> **Epilogue**
>
> *If you're feeling mentally fatigued, step away from the decision-making table and go for a change of scenery, activity, perspective, or just some good old rest and relaxation.*

71

Go Have Fun!

Yep! That's right. Go have fun! When your thinking process is tapped out, get up and go have a good time.

If you're at work, go find a favorite coworker and have a lighthearted chat. No talking business though, unless it's to good-naturedly poke fun at the situation. Or, you could close your office door, close the blinds, put on your favorite music, and dance up a storm. Yes! People really do these things—and they work! Sometimes letting yourself go and being a little silly can unlock something in you. After all, it takes a lot of energy and brainpower to always be "on."

If you're home, the dancing thing is even more

> **Assignment**
>
> Go have fun!

likely, but you could also spend some time reading a good book. Or, you could catch that favorite flick you've been waiting to see, or pop in your favorite DVD. The point is to stop and let yourself be entertained.

Get the family in on the act. If it's quitting time at the office, call your spouse and meet for dinner somewhere. Or order pizza and enjoy a ferocious family Scrabble tournament.

It doesn't matter what you choose to do, as long as it's good, clean fun. In a short time you'll see how it's also productive fun. You'll return to that tough decision refreshed and with renewed vigor to tackle and conquer it. And when you've done that, feel free to reward yourself with a little victory dance!

Epilogue
All work and no play make you a dull-minded person!

72

Sweat It Out!

Sweating through a tough decision? Then throw on your workout clothes and start sweating for real.

A 2004 study conducted by researchers at the University of Illinois shows that exercise can improve brain activity in people of all ages, from children to senior adults.

So if you're struggling with a mental block, get yourself moving. A brisk walk can do wonders for clearing your head. Heck, you can even take the dog along—if you must multitask. Or, if you're into running, roller blading, or playing tennis, get going. Just do something to get your blood pumping, push more oxygen through your system, refresh and reinvigorate your brain cells.

Assignment

Stop trying to sweat through mental fatigue! Instead, get up and exercise your way to a clearer head and more powerful sense of self.

Exercising can do more for your mind than just improve your oxygen levels. It can also give you a sense of being physically powerful. Let's face it: when you're mentally fatigued, you can start to feel powerless. In fact, the feeling of powerlessness is the root cause of frustration.

Epilogue

Work through a mental block with a good physical workout.

73

Go Mindless!

If you've been running on all four cylinders of brainpower, then slam on the breaks and go mindless—by doing something that doesn't use much brainpower at all.

That could be washing the dishes, vacuuming, cleaning your desk, or straightening your files. The point is to choose something that you can do on autopilot.

Stay clear of activities that require you to make choices or analyze anything. To go mindless means to do something you're so familiar with you could do it in your sleep.

Scientists have found that switching from heavy-duty thinking to more routine tasks

Assignment

Clean your desk, wash the dishes, or do something routine that doesn't require you to think about it.

is similar to flipping a circuit breaker. You go from grappling in the dark with a decision to suddenly finding the solution bathed in a whole new light.

In fact, the sense of accomplishment you get from completing a routine task can restart your confidence, dissolve your frustration, and clear your head. And the best part about going mindless is that you don't have to go mindless for long. A half hour of switching gears can be enough for most people to give their brains a rest and get back into the action.

Epilogue

When you've hit a mental block, power down your brain and switch to something more routine and mindless.

74

Give It a Rest!

Sometimes nothing will break through the haze of mental fatigue except rest—or a good night's sleep.

If you're finding yourself snapping at others, your patience thinning, and your body dragging, you're fighting a losing battle. Give it a rest!

How much rest you need really depends on the situation. If you're not too far gone, a half hour looking out of your office window could be enough to recharge your batteries. But if you've been tossing a decision around in your head and analyzing scenario after scenario for hours, then call it quits for the day as soon as possible. Go home, kick your feet up, have a good meal, possibly a glass of wine, watch a good movie, and go to bed.

Assignment

Take a rest from the problem. It will recharge you mentally, physically, emotionally, and spiritually.

In fact, giving it a rest—a real rest—means you forbid yourself to even think about the decision until you get back into the office the next day.

Wallowing in a decision does not get you closer to overcoming mental fatigue; it only exacerbates it. Why make life tough on yourself by continuing to push further than you can mentally go at the time? If you're tapped out, you're tapped out.

Epilogue

When you're too far gone with mental fatigue, give yourself a rest. Face the fact squarely; when you're tapped out, you're tapped out.

75

Try Some Theory

When you've come to a mental block on the road to a decision, take a side trip into a little theory.

Now, if you're the type that is put off by the word "theory," thinking it is something only useful in academia but has no place in the day-to-day reality of business, you need to change your thinking.

It's from theory that some of mankind's greatest achievements have germinated. Space travel. It was once just a theory. A cure for tuberculosis. It was once a theory. Invitro fertilization for childless couples. It was also once a mere theory.

All of these theories have been realized today, and all because someone took time to consider them and put them into practice.

Still put off by the word theory? Then try this example. It was during the Apollo 13 mission that the theory of re-booting the ship's computer system saved the astronauts' lives. This was the first time a computer was rebooted. If someone had not taken a side trip into theory, and used it to

> ### *Assignment*
>
> When you're con-fronted with a mental block, get out of the tried-and-true and take a little adventure in theory.

make a critical decision on that fateful mission, lives would have been lost—and who knows if the U.S. space program would have survived until today.

The lesson here is that theory is preparation for possibility.

> ### Epilogue
> *Good decision makers embrace theory as the prepara-tion of possibility.*

76

Who's That Cheerleader in the Cute Outfit?

You are not done once the decision is made, so don't rest comfortably.

Now you need to commu-nicate your decision to others and "sell" the decision. Your task changes from one of de-cision maker to decision implementer. And the first step

> ### *Assignment*
>
> Begin honing your communication skills. You need to communi-cate the decision.

in that process is to communicate the decision in the best possible terms.

That makes you a cheerleader. You are the one who made the decision, or headed up the group who made the decision, so it is incumbent upon you to communicate that decision to others. And you know you made a good decision, so you need to communicate that decision positively.

Epilogue

A decision that is not communicated well is a decision that may not be implemented effectively.

77

You Can Be a Cheerleader

So you become the cheerleader for the decision. You have to "sell" the decision to everyone else.

If you made the decision yourself (autocratic method) then you are alone in this process. If you lead a group to consensus, then you have the group to aid you in this process. But now you are the sales force for the decision, and there are some key things you need to accomplish:

- ◆ Make certain the decision is communicated to everyone at the same time.

- ◆ Make certain everyone affected gets the word.

Assignment

Keep a list of the key points so you can reinforce them on other communication occasions.

♦ Make certain you are thorough in your presentation of the details about what the problem was and why the solution was selected.

♦ Make certain you communicate most of this personally, not indirectly via letters and newsletters.

♦ Make certain you discuss the consequences of the decision and the expected outcomes.

♦ Highlight the positive and address the negative (if any).

Epilogue

A decision that is badly communicated will not be well received, and may well result in lowered morale and decreased productivity.

78

Being Supportive of Other Decision Makers

As a decision maker yourself, you need to recognize others have similar responsibilities. If you want them to support your decisions, you have to be supportive of their decisions as well.

When a fellow manager makes and announces a decision, be sure to support him or

Assignment

Make sure you have good relationships with other managers and decision makers in your organization and you support their decisions.

99

her publicly and offer any assistance he or she might need in implementation. Do that visibly so others will notice. Help your colleague implement the decision.

Why? Because when you make decisions, you want their support as well. Having your fellow managers and decision makers aiding you in implementation can make all the difference in the world in the decision's ultimate effectiveness. But if you don't help, don't expect help from them.

Epilogue
Implementing a decision effectively requires help. Make certain your fellow decision makers will help.

79

Learn From Others' Experiences

If you are inexperienced at decision making, observe and learn from others. Watch how they go about the process of making decisions, and watch the results and outcomes.

If you have some experience yourself, but need help, rely on more experienced or other managers to share their experiences with you.

There are few problems, challenges, or opportunities that have not happened in some way in the past. That

Assignment
Keep mentors and other experienced decision makers available for counsel.

means there are people out there who have experience with them. Try to tap into that experience and learn from it.

One way to do that is to have a couple of good professional mentors available to talk to when you face key decisions.

> ### Epilogue
> *Part of learning how to make good decisions comes from learning from others' experiences.*

80

Respecting Differences of Opinion

As you gather information and get others' opinions, remember that you are the honest broker at this point. Any opinion is a good opinion. Any recommendation is a good recommendation. While you might not eventually decide to use any of these opinions or recommendations, they are always given to help.

Be respectful of the time and effort others take to provide you with their opinions on your decision. After all, you have asked and you will probably ask again in the future. If they think you are not taking their opinions seriously, they will not be so helpful in the future.

> ### Assignment
>
> You can remember when someone asked your opinion and then ignored it. Did it feel good?

And just because you might not make the decision the way another has recommended this time, it doesn't mean you might not do so in the future.

> ### Epilogue
> *Respect the recommendations and opinions of others. They are always valuable.*

81

Handling Other Decision Makers

Remember that often your decisions will affect other decision makers in some way. While you should, as we have discussed, always consult with other decision makers, the decision is yours to make. But if it has an affect on other decision makers, then you have some additional steps to take.

First, once the decision is made, inform them first and brief them on why the decision was made that way. Second, consider their comments and observations. It's your final line of defense. Finally, consider their concerns and make accommodations as you can, especially if your decision has an affect on them or their responsibilities.

Remember: these people are important to your success with this decision.

> ### *Assignment*
>
> Think about others once the decision is made, especially fellow decision makers.

Take care of them and their concerns. If you need to make some minor modifications to your decision, consider that as a way of accommodating others in your organization. You will be seen as a team player as a result, and be trusted by other decision makers as a consequence.

Epilogue
Other decision makers are important to you. Handle them effectively.

82

Handling Those Affected by the Decision

Decisions affect lots of people: your employees, your boss, decision makers and divisions of your organization, and anyone who does business with you or your organization.

Your decision may have an affect on these people. As a manager, recall that you have a responsibility not only to consider them as you make the decision, but also to consider communicating with them once the decision has been made. And you must do this effectively, not just by direction.

One way to think about this is to "sell" your decision to others. Not sell as in actually making them want to buy it, but sell in the sense of explaining why the decision was made, the way it was made, and why the expected outcomes of the decision will be better for the organization. Along the way, point out why the outcomes will be generally better for everyone involved.

This requires good communication skills, but the most important skill is the willingness to address everyone honestly and directly. Speak personally with employees. Meet with fellow managers. Brief your boss personally and first. Provide people outside your organization with the information in the most appropriate way available; consult your public relations or sales personnel on this one.

Assignment

Recall when changes were made in other organizations and you never got the word? It came as a surprise. Did you like that?

103

> ### Epilogue
> *Inform everyone fully and completely once the decision is made.*

83

Handling Your Own Staff

If there is a group that you cannot ignore, it's your staff or your employees. After all, you consulted with them while making the decision, and they know something is coming. And more often than not, they will be the ones who will have to implement the decision.

So, handle this communication well and appropriately. Speak to them personally as a group. Be detailed in your explanation of how you came to the decision. Remind them you consulted with them. Explain clearly how the decision will benefit the organization (and them, if it will).

> ### *Assignment*
>
> Recall a decision made without subsequent detailed instructions on how to implement it. Did it work?

Finally, make certain you present them with their specific roles in helping to implement the decision. Ultimately, this is where the rubber meets the road. Your employees will be the ones to implement this decision, and they need to have your guidance on just how to do that. Be as detailed as necessary. Involve them, if you can, in the actual implementation process. Remember: they are the ones on the front lines of your organization, making your products or serving your customers. They can be invaluable resources in making this decision successful.

Epilogue

Employees are your decision implementers, so make sure they are part of the execution process.

84

Be "Ask Assertive," Not "Tell Assertive"

When communicating the decision to others, the real authoritarian style would be to take the army sergeant approach: "Okay, that's my decision. I don't care if you don't like it, just do it."

That might work for the Army sergeant (I doubt it works very often!), but it will not work for most of us. Instead of "telling" people what to do, we should be asking them to support the decision willingly. That's the difference between "tell assertive," when we simply tell people the decision and expect them to execute it, and "ask assertive," when we ask them to participate in executing the decision.

One of the biggest differences is that ask-assertive people will not only brief everyone on the decision, but also explain how and why the decision was made. Then they will ask everyone to help make it work by willingly executing the decision.

Assignment

Recall decisions you had forced on you. Were you enthusiastic about them?

Authoritarians will use tell assertive style, not explain the why and how, expect everyone to like it, and enthusiastically execute the decision.

But we know from long years of experience and research that people are much more willing to execute a decision if they know why and how the decision was made, and if they are asked to step forward and help make that decision work.

Epilogue

Those who use the authoritarian style usually run into opposition to the decision. As a result, it's often not executed well.

85

Show Them, Don't Tell Them

Consider, as you make your decision and as you determine how it is to be executed, your position as manager. You are also a role model. People will look to you and your behaviors as models of how to be a good employee of the organization.

Thus, once a decision is made, don't just tell people about it, model any behaviors it involves personally. Set the standard, and allow others to watch you make this decision happen.

If you decide, for example, to accept any return from customers no matter what the reason (and assuming this is a change from the usual 20-questions routine customers get), then spend the first day on the front lines handling all the returns.

Assignment

Remember those "do as I say, not as I do" managers? Want to be one of them?

Show your staff how to handle returns with the new behaviors simply by exhibiting them yourself in front of them.

Epilogue

Role modeling is an important function of managers. Be one.

86

When You Don't Have the Final Decision

Even CEOs don't always have the final decision. Often, they must follow the direction of their board, stockholders, government, and sometimes even the public.

Assignment

Determine the level of influence you could have regarding a problem or issue by considering what knowledge and expertise you can lend to the situation.

So, if you find yourself having to defer the final decision to someone else or a group, resist the temptation to take it as an insult to your competency. Remember that rarely do the most powerful players have carte blanche to make critical decisions without a higher authority's approval.

But that doesn't mean you can't play an influential role in the final decision. You can be the person that frames the issue, researches the situation, and provides the pros and cons, and other "intelligence" to the final decision maker.

In doing this, you position yourself as a leader on the issue, if not an expert. Following this approach, it is more likely than

107

not that your input and opinion on the matter will be valued and heard. If you've done your homework, it will show—and it could earn you a place at the table when the final decision is made.

Influence can sometimes be a more powerful card to hold than final decision-making authority.

Epilogue

Even when you don't have the final decision, you can leverage your knowledge and leadership on an issue to play an influential role in the final outcome.

87

Power Versus Influence

Experts describe influence in many ways. But one view is similar: influence is a skill of leadership. In fact, it's been said that influence is the greatest of all human skills.

Influence is about moving people to action or change. And those who have influence have something more powerful than power itself.

Power is one muscle people flex to start change. Often, that means flexing status or authority, but influence is different from power because it's more carrot than stick, and more sustainable and lasting over time.

In most cases, power is hard influence, meaning that people feel forced into taking action or making a change. With hard influence, people come to a set of behaviors or actions out of fear of a consequence, such as "I might lose my job."

But soft influence, which is the most powerful and sustainable over the long haul, drives action or a change in people's behavior based on its own merits. In other words, soft influence uses ration and reason over rank or status. The techniques of good decision making are all grounded in soft influence.

Assignment

To practice soft influence, you will need to listen, gather information, weigh the pros and cons of a situation, and make a reasonable case for the decision at hand.

Epilogue

Soft influence is the power of ration and reason over rank and status.

88

Practicing Reason Over Rank for Better Decisions

Remember back to a time when someone was trying to persuade you to believe their way of thinking? Were they successful at getting you to voluntarily buy in? Or did they have to pull rank?

With so many organizations using consensus gathering to come to decisions, the need to use reason over rank is more important than ever. And the forced go-along-to-get-along approach doesn't stand a chance in consensus gathering.

When we take the time to help others see how our thinking makes sense in a given situation, we have significantly better odds of being successful. Often, people pull rank because they have lost patience in trying to get others to see their way of thinking; or they have not given their proposed idea the forethought to anticipate questions, find gaps in their thinking and fill them, or to carefully, yet succinctly, articulate their viewpoint.

Pulling rank is usually an outcrop of frustration, and it usually sows resentment and resistance. And through time, those feelings compound with people and can destroy your credibility with others.

> ### Assignment
>
> Use ration and reasoning to develop partnerships in decision making.

But reason is the result of sound thinking and confidence in that thinking, which usually reaps buy-in and support. In short, reason brings partnership, which builds up the emotional bank account with your colleagues and superiors.

> ### Epilogue
> *Reason takes time and quality thinking, but it trumps rank in group decision making.*

89

Win-Win Is an Easy Sell

A win-win approach can make you a winner in selling your ideas. When people believe you have their interests at heart, and you are open about your own, you set the stage for trust. Remember that people buy in to ideas and people they trust.

If you've come to the table determined to find a win-win, your focus will be squarely on that goal, rather than pushing your own ideas. That means you will need to take a page out of author Stephen Covey's *The 7 Habits of Highly Effective People* and "seek first to understand." Simply put, you will need to focus on others before you can "seek to be understood," and start lobbying your own ideas.

> ### *Assignment*
>
> Take a lesson from good salespeople, who know that learning what their customers need and fulfilling those needs is the most successful route to making the sale.

Yet ironically, when you show you genuinely want to help others in the group get what they want, you'll find that most people are willing to give you what you want. Yes, it seems counterintuitive, but if you have reasonable requests and realistic expectations, you will be pleasantly surprised at how accommodating others are willing to be—and how easily you can accomplish a win-win.

> ### Epilogue
> *If you apply the same practice in decision making, you'll be a winner at getting others to buy in to your ideas.*

90

Evaluating Decisions

Warning! What you're about to read can make you a highly successful decision maker. But it takes professional courage and dedication to learning.

After your decisions have been implemented, you'll need to evaluate them. Were they good decisions, bad decisions, or somewhere in between? Did you get the result you planned on? Or did results fall short of the goal?

Facing the truth about our decisions takes courage, and that kind of bravery is not as prevalent in organizations as you might think. Looking our decisions square in the eye after the fact is scary, because we don't want to see any shortcomings or failures.

> ### Assignment
>
> From the onset of your decision-making efforts, have a plan on how you'll evaluate the success of that decision.

But by evaluating the outcome of our decisions, we learn how to be better the next time around. We learn from success what worked, and from failure what didn't. We also learn from those results what falls into the range of mediocrity.

If we fail in this critical step of decision-making, we may find ourselves left out of opportunity all together, down the road.

> ### Epilogue
>
> *Author and poet Maya Angelou once said: "There are no mistakes, only lessons." And that's exactly how you should view the outcome of your decisions.*

91

Evaluation Also Means Looking at People

In most decision-making situations, you are often asked to not only make a decision about the what, but also about the who. Who will execute the decision? Who will manage the effort? Who will report to whom about what?

When you look at the success or failure of your decision, also look at how well the people you placed into positions executed their roles. Did you select the right people for the right jobs? Did they meet expectations? Were they provided with the tools to execute the decision successfully? Did the put the energy and intellectual effort into the outcome that was appropriate?

People are critical to making decisions work. When you evaluate outcomes, evaluate your decisions in light of the people you placed in positions to affect the decision's outcomes. Don't discount their efforts. People can often make a bad decision a success through outstanding effort, or make a great decision fail through lack of effort on incompetence.

Assignment

Go back and review some old decisions—ones either you or someone else made. What can you learn?

Epilogue

People are important to every decision you are involved in making. They often mean success or failure. Choose wisely!

92

Good Decisions Today Are Tomorrow's Successes Replayed

When you make good decisions, you set yourself up for success again and again. Each time you make a successful decision, and the outcomes prove it, you have a model to follow and experience to reflect back on when presented with future decisions.

But good decisions come about through good planning, knowing how to create a win-win through soft influence, and being able to evaluate how successful a decision was compared with the goals and objectives first established.

Frankly, if you master the elements of good decision making, and later delegation (which is the implementation of decisions), you'll prove to yourself and others that you are true leadership material. You won't have to tell anyone, or brag, or flash your resume around. You and the people around you will see. In short, the results will speak for themselves.

Assignment

Learn and practice the ideas presented in this book.

A successful track record of good judgment is built one decision at a time. And each one that delivers the expected result brings more opportunity to be included in more decision making. With so many professionals today clamoring to be "at the table," it is—more often than not—the proven leaders that get invited.

Epilogue

Master the elements of good decision making and you'll prove yourself worthy of being called leadership material.

93

Moving On—From Sucess and Failure

When a decision has been a success, note what made it so, revel in it, and then get ready for the next one. Remember, good leaders have a track record of good decisions, and they know that one good decision does not a success make. Instead, it is the accumulation of multiple good decisions that give them the confidence and knowledge to keep making them again and again.

> **Assignment**
>
> Whether your decision was ultimately a success or failure, you need to learn from both, and keep both in healthy perspective.

But though you will certainly want to strive to always make the right decision, the fact is no one is ever 100 percent. Let's face it; even professional baseball players strive for a batting average of only 30 to 40 percent—and *they* make the big bucks.

If you serve in a decision-making role long enough, you will stumble. It is inevitable. And just as you would want to revel for a short time in a successful decision, you don't want to wallow in the failures. They are going to happen.

The best way to handle failed decisions is to treat them like the successes: note what made them failures, learn from them, and get ready for the next one. And if you apply what you learn to that next one, you will greatly reduce the risk of repeating the past.

115

Epilogue

Just as you want to revel for a short time in the limelight of a good decision, you also don't want to wallow in the disappointment of a failed one. Learn, grow—and move on!

94

Defining Delegation

Once the decisions have been made, it's time to get to work. But you can't do it all yourself. And if you think you can, you're wrong. In fact, doing it all yourself can burn you out, dull your decision-making skills, and make you the weak link in the team's drive for success.

You need to delegate! But just what is delegation?

Delegation is sharing the load. It's about communicating the vision for success, setting clear direction, and then assigning responsibilities based on the project needs and your employees' abilities.

Whether you're the CEO of a Fortune 500 company, a small-business owner or a homemaker, you can put delegation to work for you. Smart CEOs delegate the operation of the business to their vice presidents, and expect them to do the same with their managers, and so on. Successful small-business owners may work more hands-on than a corporate CEO, but they also know how to spread responsibilities among their

> **Assignment**
>
> Read the ideas on delegation and learn the difference between working hard and working smart.

employees. And balanced homemakers know how to get the family in on the act of managing the household.

It really doesn't matter what size organization you are with, or if your with an organization at all: when it's time to get the work done, it's time to delegate.

Epilogue

When it's time to get the work done, you need to delegate!

95

Delegation Versus Decision Making

Delegation and decision making are both equally important when it comes to getting things done quickly and successfully, whether at the office or at home. But they are not the same.

Decision making is about determining the direction you're going to take. Delegation is about developing the road map and selecting the vehicles you'll use to reach your destination.

In short, decision making is the *what*, while delegation is the *how*. Of course, even when you're delegating, you'll have to make decisions along the way, such as to whom and what you'll delegate. But the overarching decision, what you'll achieve, must be determined before you can delegate any of the work at hand.

Yet decision making and delegation share two things in common: authority and accountability. For your decisions to be valid, you must have been given the authority to make them. And you're also responsible for the outcomes of your decisions.

The same is true when delegating. For people to follow your direction, they must see you as having the proper authority

117

to do the delegating. And you'll be responsible for the results your team achieves, based on how and to whom you've delegated. Though some key decisions may be yours and yours alone, delegation is never a one-man show.

> ### Assignment
>
> Learn the difference between decision making and delegation and you'll be off to a good start in the right direction.

> ### Epilogue
>
> *While decision making is the what, and can sometimes be a road you travel alone, delegation is the how, and it's never a one-man show.*

96

What Delegation Is Not

So now that you know what delegation is, let's talk about what it is not.

Delegation is not abdicating your authority or your responsibility to be accountable. Nor is it about pushing off unfavorable tasks onto subordinate employees. It is also not flexing your "boss muscle" to show that you're large and in charge and have free reign to order others around.

Delegation is also not about setting others up to fail by delegating tasks to them that you know to be far beyond their capabilities. Neither is delegation about playing favorites and giving the spotlight tasks consistently to only one or two employees, while leaving the others with the unrecognized grunt work.

Unloading, shuffling tasks off to employees when you're overwhelmed or bored, is not effective delegation either. And it's not about flying by the seat of your pants, meaning if you're going to delegate, you better have a plan and your employees need to fully understand it.

But just as delegation is not about giving up authority and accountability, it's also not about giving up power and control. And finally, delegation is not a sign of weakness, or your inability to do it all. In fact, if you're trying to do it all, you are sure to fail—and your team right along with you.

> **Assignment**
>
> Make certain you understand what delegation is not. That will save you trouble later.

> **Epilogue**
> *Delegation is not about giving up your authority, power, control, accountability, or your responsibility to help your employees succeed.*

97

Organizational Culture—Are You Set Up to Succeed?

Effective delegation does not occur in a vacuum. Your organization or household culture has a big influence on how effectively you can delegate.

For example, some organizations praise managers for empowering their employees and encourage them to reward and recognize initiative—an environment that is ripe for delegating. Yet, some organizations encourage micromanagement and martyrdom among their leaders, creating an environment that screams: "If you want it done right, do it yourself."

But also look beyond the management mentality in your organization to that of the rank-and-file employees. Are employees motivated and driven to take initiative? Or is your organization dominated by a bargaining unit, such as a union, that discourages employees from doing anything beyond their immediate job description.

For you to fully bring delegation to your work, you have to be in a workplace that will allow you to succeed. If employees are discouraged from stretching and growing beyond their current capabilities, or if your management does not trust the workforce, it will be difficult to practice the more ideal techniques of delegation.

> ## Assignment
>
> Know your organization's culture so you can determine how you will need to approach delegation as a whole.

But even if your company's culture is less than optimal for delegating, practicing even some degree of delegation is better than none at all.

> ### Epilogue
> *High-performance work cultures are prime for delegation. But even if yours is less than ideal, some degree of delegation will still make you more effective than not delegating at all.*

98

A Closer Look at Delegation

Because management sets the example and sculpts the work environment, it is important to take a look around you—to your management peers to the right and left of you, and to those above and below you.

Do those to the left and the right model delegation? Are they open to delegating to one another, and to one another's staff members? This is known as sideways delegation, and it's completely acceptable where management works as teams, rather than in department silos.

Also consider if managers below you are encouraged to delegate as well, and if upper management rewards good delegation practices. If the answer is yes to either of these, it

Assignment

If your company's management culture supports delegation through encouragement, recognition, and equality, then read on and get to delegating. But if you see some gaps or imbalances in how your management views delegation, read on and consider carefully how to proceed.

is very likely you can be confident that your management will support you in your effort to delegate work.

But don't stop there. Take a look around at the men and women in your management ranks. Does your company send different signals about delegation to men versus women, and vice versa? In some organizations, male managers are expected to delegate, but female managers are the recipients of delegated work from their male counterparts. However, the reverse can also be true, in which male managers can be criticized by female superiors for delegating work.

Epilogue

Your company's management sets the tone for delegation. Do your homework and find the right formula for delegating— one that will work in your unique company culture.

99

Delegating Sideways and Upward

If you thought delegating was only one dimensional, think again. Delegation can be an equal-opportunity practice, meaning you can delegate sideways and upward, in addition to downward.

Say what? Delegating sideways and upward? You mean delegating to my boss and Joe the marketing manager in the office next door? Yep!

Again, it will take some homework on your part to determine if sideways and upward delegation are acceptable in your work culture. If you find they are, get with it! But remember, delegation is never about shuffling work off on someone else, and sideways and upward delegating are no different.

> ### *Assignment*
> Look around you to determine when and where sideways and upward delegation are appropriate and feasible.

So how do you delegate to your management peers or to your boss? Think about who is most capable of getting the job done quickly. For instance, if you're struggling with a decision that seems outside of your experience, consult with your boss. Her experience may give you insight that can drastically reduce the thought needed to arrive at a final conclusion. The same with your management peers. They may have reports, analysis, and insights that can help you come to a decision quickly.

> ### Epilogue
> *View delegation as an equal-opportunity practice and delegate sideways and upward.*

100

Why Delgate?

The ability to delegate is the litmus test of good leadership. Managers that can delegate well will separate themselves from the management pack—and stand out as organizational leaders. Why is that, you ask? Because when delegation is done right it shares opportunity, provides a sense of achievement, and enables others to develop themselves through new experiences.

Let's start with the notion of sharing opportunity. Good leaders need to be focused on achieving the big picture, setting the direction, and ensuring employees have what they need to succeed. And part of succeeding is having opportunity—the chance to contribute to the big picture, to make a difference. Delegation provides opportunities for your employees to be part of something bigger than themselves.

The contributions of each individual add up, and with good leadership at the helm, they collectively lead to a sense of accomplishment for the whole group. That sense of achievement is a more powerful motivator than money. That's right! Study after study has shown that money is a fleeting motivator, but a sense of accomplishment is the highest-sustaining motivator for employees.

> ### *Assignment*
>
> Delegate responsibilities to your employees and, in turn, provide them with experiences to grow and stretch themselves as professionals and people.

Delegation also offers a chance for self-development. It's a known fact that we learn best through our direct experiences. When you provide this opportunity, it can be a gift that keeps on giving throughout your employees' lives, and it can pay big dividends for your reputation as a leader and a professional.

123

> **Epilogue**
>
> *Delegating can provide opportunity, a sense of achievement, a chance for employees to develop themselves, and a prime opportunity for you to stand out as a true leader.*

101

But I'll Be Giving Up Power!

Giving up power is one of the common barriers to good delegation—and it is the most irrational. Refusing to delegate actually makes you power*less*.

Power does not come from hoarding the work. In fact, thinking you can do it all, and acting along those lines, fails to show that you can lead. And if you're a manager, you're expected to lead.

True power in leadership doesn't come from personally accomplishing the work. It comes from your ability to develop your staff and motivate them to achieve strategic ends. It

> ### *Assignment*
>
> Remember this! Your thinking and discipline is the real power source behind your team's success.

comes from aligning people's capabilities with the tasks at hand, and using work opportunities to build their confidence, project after project.

When you think of delegation, think of a ship captain. Rarely does the captain row the boat. His job is to see out across the horizon, set the course, and ensure the boat is moving in the right direction toward the charted destination.

It is not the power behind the oars or the ship's wheel that gets the boat to where it is supposed to go. It is the thinking and discipline—the leadership—that makes it happen.

Epilogue

Refusing to delegate makes you powerless because true power in leadership doesn't come from personally accomplishing the work.

102

Get More Time to Get More Done

Time is at a premium for everyone today. Let's face it—24 hours is just not enough time to get it all done. And with businesses today pressed to do more with less, employees are stretched to the maximum.

But delegation can be your ticket for getting more time to get things done. For example, you may have four meetings scheduled in one day, but you still have to meet the deadline for completing the conference

Assignment

Pick those tasks that absolutely must have your attention and delegate the rest.

marketing plan. If this is enough to make your heart start racing and your head swimming—stop!

That's right. With all that you have to do and in such little time, stop—but just long enough to ask yourself if you really have to be at the meetings? Can one of your staff members attend one or two of the meetings and brief you afterward? Or can a coworker attend on your behalf?

It is true that 80 percent of success is just showing up. But you have to balance that against another adage: pick your battles. The same is true in prioritizing your work.

Epilogue

Delegating effectively means you have to put your focus where it should truly be, a practice that can give you more time to get more done—and all from the same 24 hours.

103

Make Quick, Quality Decisions

Have you ever heard yourself say: "I just need time to get my hands around this?" Or felt you had so much to do you couldn't focus long enough to give decisions quality thought?

Well, you're not alone. In a world where everyone is expected to do more with less, it is easy to feel like your attention is pulled in several different directions. In fact, if you had the time to think straight, and good information to work from, you could find better ways to do even more with less. Right?

Once again, delegation can be the cure for this thought-depleting disease of doing more with less. How? By delegating, you push decisions to those who are

Assignment

Delegate select decision-making responsibilities and tasks to the right people, and give yourself the luxury of delivering quicker, quality decisions that could buy you greater efficiency, effectiveness, and more time!

closest to the work and who are often very familiar with processes and practices that can hinder your team's ability to do more with less. Relying on those who are closest to the work to make key decisions based on expectations and direction you've established, can result in quicker and better quality decisions.

But that's not the only benefit. Delegating decisions and responsibilities to those on the front lines allows you more time to think. Yes—delegating will give you time to stop and think, review critical reports and plans, and hold crucial conversations with your management peers and superiors.

Epilogue

Delegating gives you quicker and better decision-making power to find better *ways to do even more with less.*

104

Employees Unite!

In management, success depends on the ability to get results through people. But to get the best results, you have to unite your employees.

Delegation provides an excellent opportunity to harness employees' talents, expertise, interests, and enthusiasm to achieve a common goal. In short, delegation is a group thing.

But delegation is about much more than just handing out assignments and responsibilities. You have to understand that all people—including your employees—want to feel a sense of purpose, to be valued, and to be part of something bigger than themselves.

Delegation can fulfill each of these needs when you assign project tasks and responsibilities based on team members' varying

127

expertise and talents. This shows you trust them, you want their involvement, and recognize what they each have to offer. It also sends the same message to others on the team and outside of the team.

When you demonstrate your employees are valued and appreciated you will increase their overall commitment to whatever it is you're working to achieve.

Assignment

Delegation is all about inclusion, and aligning employees to a common goal. Tap into what motivates and drives them, and play to the touch points of each employee. If you do this, you'll not only have mastered delegation, but you'll likely transform your team to all-around stellar performers.

Epilogue
Helen Keller once said, "Alone we achieve little, but together we can achieve much." Delegation is a group thing.

105

Encourage Employee Commitment

If you approach delegation as a group thing, you're more likely to get greater commitment from your employees. And commitment has always been the true differentiator between winning and losing.

By pushing decisions to the front lines, employees become part of the process—instead of having the process imposed on them. And let's face it, no one likes to have something mandated to them. In fact, participation is a cardinal rule in change management. Leave employees out of the decision to implement a new change, and you'll likely have a modest revolt on your hands, at best.

But give them an active role that shows you value their knowledge and experience, and you'll likely generate enthusiastic dedication that could drive you to results beyond your expectations.

Assignment

Remember this! All people want to be part of something greater than themselves. With delegation, you can give your employees that opportunity everyday.

Epilogue

Give employees an active role in key decisions and tasks and you'll generate enthusiastic commitment that could deliver success beyond your expectations.

106

Teach a Man to Fish

If you've always thought of delegation as just a way to help you get more done, then here is an opportunity to expand your thinking.

Delegation provides you with the opportunity to practice servant leadership, which is using your authority and responsibility to serve those who work for you. You see, delegation is not just about serving your needs as the manager—it is also about growing your employees personally and professionally. Good leaders learn this quickly in their careers.

When you give employees an active role, you give them an opportunity to learn, and learning gives them lifelong skills and a foundation of experience upon which they can continue to build their careers. In essence, you can use delegation to teach them to fish for a lifetime.

Assignment

Using delegation to teach your employees to fish is a win-win situation all the way around.

But you don't have to be a philanthropist to embrace the advantages of servant leadership. Teaching your employees to fish, through delegation, is an investment that will deliver success to your organization both in the short and long term.

What they learn through delegation can be applied to bring greater efficiencies and effectiveness to the job, and elevates the employee's experience from which you can continue to build. In marketing, this is known as the efficiency curve, in which the organization increases profits because employees use their learning to make more product or deliver better services at lower and lower operational costs over time.

Epilogue

Take a servant-leadership approach to delegation, using it as an opportunity to teach your employees to fish for themselves professionally and personally.

107

Know Your Management Style

Do you know your management style? If not, find out. Some management styles are more conducive to delegating than others. But also be prepared to adjust your management style depending on the employee to which you're delegating.

For example, is your management style authoritarian, meaning you determine the who, what, when, and how of the work, with little prior input from employees? This is known as a tell-assertive style of management in which there is little employee participation in the decision-making phase of the task.

Or is your style more of that of a team leader, meaning you gather input from staff and encourage them to participate in the decision-making process? This is a more ask-assertive style of management.

Good leaders learn to vary their management styles, and thus delegating approaches, based on an employee's level of experience, knowledge, teamwork skills, and readiness to accept supervision.

Employees with high levels of experience and knowledge, who work well with others and readily accept their supervision, will work more effectively under a team-leader management style. And they are a prime group to whom you can delegate tasks *and* decisions.

However, employees with limited experience and knowledge, or who have

Assignment

Know your management style and be prepared to adjust it when delegating to employees with differing levels of experience, knowledge, teamwork skills, and acceptance of supervision.

difficulty working in a team or accepting supervision, are more effectively managed through a tell-assertive style. They need closer supervision and direction. You will need to carefully consider what tasks to delegate to this group, and may delay delegating any decision-making responsibilities until teamwork and acceptance of supervision improve.

Epilogue

Good leaders vary their management and delegation styles based on their employees' experiences.

108

Develop Your Coaching Skills

To delegate effectively, you'll need well-developed coaching skills. But what is a coach?

A coach in the workplace is just like a coach on the court. She assesses her team's individual skills and how they work together as a group, determines who is the best fit for completing specifics tasks and making relevant decisions. But that's just the beginning.

Assignment

Remember this! Coaching requires tremendous forethought and interpersonal skills, but the outcome of both is effective delegation.

To coach effectively, you'll need to be clear on what you expect when your employee undertakes a project or decision, and review practices and procedures that will help him be successful along the way. You'll even want to review possible problem scenarios and how the employee should handle those. And finally, you'll want to observe and give corrective input along the way to keep the employee on track.

And don't skip this final step of giving corrective input. It may be uncomfortable to provide constructive criticism, but it's absolutely necessary. As basketball coaching great John Wooden says: "A coach is someone who can give correction without causing resentment." When corrective input is given with the clear intent to help someone succeed, it is also a demonstration of good coaching skills.

Epilogue

Coaching is an investment. If you give it, you will reap the dividends.

109

They Like Me! They Really Like Me!

Do your employees have to like you for delegation to work within your team? Not necessarily.

"Like" is a fleeting state of mind. It is just not possible to maintain popularity with your employees in every situation or with every single individual. To strive for that scenario is to set yourself up for failure—and the mission of your organization as well. After all, if you end up trying to please everyone, you please no one. And losing faith with your boss, your stockholders, or consumers in exchange for popularity among your employees can severely cripple your company.

But developing a good rapport with your employees encourages trust and loyalty. In fact, you'll need that trust and loyalty for delegation to work effectively within your team. Your em-

> ### *Assignment*
>
> Focus on earning your employees' respect, rather than their popular vote.

ployees have to trust that you're fair and consistent in dealing with issues and team conflicts. They also will need to feel confident that you will loyally back them if something beyond their control goes wrong.

In short, employees are more apt to "like" you if you're authentic, fair, and consistent—all the ingredients of true integrity.

Epilogue

You will need your employees' trust and loyalty— elements of respect—to effectively delegate.

110

Popularity Is a Plus

If you find you are popular among your employees, and that popularity has been earned through your integrity, you'll likely find delegation easy to implement.

Human resource experts have found that employees' motivation and job satisfaction are tied directly to the relationship with their supervisor. And happy employees tend to be committed, enthusiastic, loyal, and eager to learn and grow. These are the attitude ingredients your employees need for delegation to work effectively.

It is worth taking the time to assess your level of popularity among your employees. An anonymous survey is an excellent way to gauge what your employees think about you as a leader.

But what if you don't get high marks from employees? View it as an opportunity, a personal and professional chal-lenge, to identify where there may be gaps in your integrity—consistency, fair-ness, authenticity—and develop a plan to fix them. Remember the words of the poet and author Maya An-gelou: "When I knew better, I did better."

Assignment

Strive to develop a hap-py team, because happy employees tend to be com-mitted, enthusiastic, loyal, and eager to learn and grow.

Epilogue

An employee's level of motivation is directly correlated to the working relationship with his supervisor.

111

Delegate to Improve Relationships

Want to increase employee satisfaction? Then get busy delegating!

Delegation is a clear act of trust if handled effectively. That show of trust is also a show of support. And sometimes showing an employee you support him can turn a poor relation-ship into a better one, and a good relationship into a great one.

Often it is mistrust that separates us from one another. But entire communities can be transformed when we let down our defenses and show a little faith in one another. The same can be true in leading employees—and delegation can provide an excellent opportunity.

But how do you get started, particularly with someone in which you have limited confidence? As au-

Assignment

Practice delegation and over time you'll find that it can be the catalyst for reversing poor employee relationships and increasing team morale overall.

thor and self-help guru Stephen Covey says, start from a point of agreement. With an employee, it can be one strength you both agree the employee demonstrates.

Select a limited task or decision that calls for that strength and delegate it to the employee. Then build from there, recognizing and rewarding the employee each time a new task is completed to your expectations.

Epilogue

Delegation is an excellent way to develop better employee relationships.

112

Authority Versus Responsibility

Authority and responsibility are similar, yet different. And when it comes to delegating, you need to know where to draw the line.

Authority is what your organization has bestowed upon you to get the job done. You give direction, and those placed under your authority are obligated to follow as part of their employment.

But authority can also include responsibilities such as signing off on budget expenditures, hiring additional staff or contract help, or approving a project to move forward.

You may delegate some of your authority, such as if you're on vacation or out of the office on business. For example, you may delegate staff management to an employee that you trust to make decisions as you would when you're away from the office.

Delegating authority means you're handing over a whole set of responsibilities encompassed within a specified level of authority. This authority may be delegated on a long- or short-term basis.

> ## Assignment
>
> Before delegating, make sure you know the difference between what is authority and what is responsibility.

But delegating responsibilities is more about assigning accountability for given tasks, often without the benefit of authority. For example, you may ask an employee to attend a weekly meeting on your behalf, but reserve your authority to make any commitments as a result of the meeting.

Epilogue

Whether you delegate authority or responsibility, you're ultimately accountable for the success or failure of the outcomes.

113

Show Them the Vision and the Rewards

Would you drive across country without knowing where you were going? Of course not! Even if you're not sure of what route you'll take, you certainly want to know your destination. Otherwise, how would you ever know when you've arrived?

The same is true when it comes to delegation.

To get the most out of delegation, show your employees the vision. Help them see what could be as a result of their efforts. For example, if your goal is to launch a new product within the next year, then show your employees what that launch will look like and what it could bring to the organization, such as increased revenues, high profits, larger bonuses for the team, and so on.

> ### Assignment
>
> To delegate effectively, begin by showing people the destination, and setting the vision of success.

And remember, vision is not exclusive to the Fortune 500 company. The same can be applied to a small business or family dynamic. A vision for a small business might be to increase productivity by 15 percent, with the pay-off being increased revenue that will help to provide insurance benefits to employees for the first time. For a family, the vision could be a larger home or dream vacation, which can be both a vision and a reward combined.

Because delegation is ultimately about sharing responsibilities and motivating others to carry them out in a way that gets results and inspires confidence, you'll need to help people see your vision.

138

Epilogue

Showing your employees the vision is to give them a view of what their efforts can create.

114

Have a Game Plan

Rarely is any endeavor successful without a plan. Christopher Columbus may not have known the final outcome of his voyage when he left the shores of Europe, but he certainly had a plan for making the journey nonetheless.

And delegation requires no less of you. All great achievements require thinking, analyzing, and preparing. When delegating, you'll need to assess your team; determine to whom you will delegate what tasks, responsibilities, and decisions; how you will get your team's buy-in and commitment; how you will set expectations and measure performance; and how you will keep your team motivated until the mission has been accomplished.

Also, if it's the first time you are delegating to an employee, plan for it to take time. You will likely need to give detailed direction the first time around, and the employee may have a number of questions up front and throughout the process.

You will also need to plan for possible failure. After all, delegating is a risk. What will you do if a team

Assignment

Having a game plan will help you think through these questions and be prepared for the journey.

139

member is not performing up to expectations? How will you adjust course if delegated decisions move the project offtrack? How will you provide feedback and realign expectations, resources, and so on?

But you will also need to plan for success. How will you recognize and reward your team members? How will you build on their experience? How will you harness the team's success and use it to drive future projects?

Epilogue
Before delegating, have a plan in place that is founded on solid thinking, analysis, and preparation.

115

The "Who" and "What" of Delegation

So, to whom should you delegate responsibilities and authority? It is probably the most important question you will ask yourself in preparing to delegate.

Yet when it comes to authority and responsibility, you're accountable for both. And that's why it is crucial for you to delegate both carefully. When delegating authority, you want to choose someone with experience, knowledge, maturity, and good interpersonal skills who is loyal and committed to the vision you've established for the team or project. In short, it should certainly be someone you trust, both in competency and character.

However, when delegating responsibilities, you'll likely need someone with the right skills and knowledge for a specific task or set of tasks. Experience, loyalty, and commitment may not always be absolute necessities when delegating responsibilities alone. In other words, you may only need to trust the employee's technical competency. But interpersonal skills may not play an important role in the task.

Assignment

Determine if you're delegating responsibilities or authority—or both. Then choose carefully who is right for the job, because in the end, you are accountable.

Regardless, however, whether you are delegating responsibilities or authority, you must trust that the person will follow all ethical, legal, and company policies. Successful delegation has no room for renegades. After all, you are accountable in the end.

Epilogue

It is crucial that you delegate both authority and responsibility carefully.

116

Assessing the Team

Once you've determined what you want to delegate, responsibilities or authority, or both, you must focus on the who. After all, it's your backside on the line if you make a wrong choice.

First, resist the urge to delegate the majority of the work to the go-getter on the team. Delegating most of the work, or worse, everything, to one person is a recipe for trouble. It sets your go-getter up for burnout and possible resentment from other team members who may feel that you're playing favorites.

Remember: Delegation is a group thing. And that means you have to share the opportunity and use it to develop your

---

Assignment

Assess employees for the job based on their past performance, their skills and expertise, and their potential for growth.

---

team as a whole. To do that, start with assessing each team member. Use performance reviews to objectively analyze team members' strengths and weaknesses, their depth of expertise, and their interest. Also use performance reviews, along with other observations you and others have made, to determine employees' development areas, such as what skills and experiences they need to help them grow.

After you've collected your input, list out the qualifications for each employee, ranging from the technical to the interpersonal, and compare them with the qualifications required for the responsibilities or authority you plan to delegate. The employee who has the most matched qualifications is likely to be your best choice.

This type of assessment may seem like a lot of work, but it is an investment that will pay off in the long run.

Epilogue

Assess the team carefully, because it's your backside on the line if you make a wrong decision.

117

Selling the Work

Selling the work requires you to get tuned into WIIFM (What's In It For Me) for your employees.

Though we would like to believe that people get behind a vision and join the mission out of pure altruism, that's just not the case. They need motivation, and nothing motivates people like knowing what they have to gain from the work you're trying to sell.

Will it result in a promotion? Will it mean more money? In short, what's the benefit to the employee? Now the Machiavellians out there would say that's easy to sell to the employee: "You'll have a job!" But coercion and management by fear gets you nowhere in the long run. Throughout time, it only builds resentment.

Assignment

To sell the work, get tuned into WIIFM with each of your employees—know what motivates each of them individually.

Before you approach the team member about the task or responsibility you're delegating to him, make a list of benefits you believe the employee will gain from taking on the responsibility. Will it help gain her exposure to senior management? Will it help him grow into a division he has been eyeing for awhile? Will it help her develop confidence in an area of work in which she is unsure?

The list you develop really depends on your knowledge of the employee and what motivates him. But if you've done your homework in assessing the team (Idea 116), then you should have good "intelligence" into how to sell the work with each individual employee.

Epilogue

Buy-in, not coercion, is the only way to successfully motivate employees.

118

Make Your Optimism Obvious

Before you can sell even one employee on the task or responsibility you're delegating, you must be convinced yourself that the person can handle the job.

If you've assessed your team thoroughly, you should have no doubt you've made the best choice with the resources you have available to you. And frankly, that is the best any manager can do in a given situation.

Trust in your assessment and selection of who should take on the task or responsibility, then make your optimism obvious. Directly spell it out to the employee: "John, I've chosen you for this role because I think you have the best knowledge and skill sets to handle this particular task."

Assignment

Directly tell your employees why they were chosen for the task or responsibility.

Sincerely showing your confidence in the employee, and your optimism about how he will handle the job, will have a powerful impact on the outcome of the task. As a manager, you have a lot to gain because your employees' success demonstrates you can effectively lead people to get results.

Epilogue

Knowing what made an employee stand out for an opportunity can be a big motivator in getting the task done, and done right.

119

Set Expectations

Pay attention to this chapter, because setting expectations is the line in the sand between success and failure in delegation. So before you delegate, you will need to have this information down solid.

First and foremost, when delegating, do not assume that your employees know what and how you want them to approach the task or responsibilities at hand. You must make it clear.

Define what role the employee should play in re-

Assignment

Be clear! Do not assume your employees know what and how you want a task completed.

lationship to the rest of the team, outline the key responsibilities you want accomplished, when you expect those to be completed, the level of authority the person will have, and what results you want to see. If the project or responsibility will be ongoing or long term, define what key milestones you want to see accomplished and, again, by what time frame and with what interim results.

To what detail you share your expectations depends on the task or responsibility you are delegating, and the competency level of the employee. Employees with higher levels of proven competency and knowledge will likely need the essentials, and may feel micromanaged if given fine details. These types of employees need room to use their own judgment and creativity, but with clear expectations of leeway and limitations.

However, employees with little experience and limited competency will need the fine details. You will have to cover more ground with these employees. But if they have detailed direction on the first task and prove to apply it correctly, they will need less and less fine detail and more essentials with future tasks.

Epilogue

You must set expectations and ensure they are clearly understood.

120

Set a Time Line

It's been said that if it weren't for the deadline, nothing would get accomplished. Just look at people filing their taxes. State revenue agencies find that half to one-third of their citizens don't file taxes until the last minute. And of course, we all remember pulling all-nighters to get that term paper finished, though we knew about it the first day of the semester.

Let's face it; it is human nature to procrastinate. That's why you need to set

Assignment

Don't let projects linger. Set key milestones and deadlines.

a time line when you delegate, so employees are very clear on what you expect in terms of meeting key milestones and deadlines.

With all the day-to-day distractions that employees experience, including yourself, it's very easy to let projects linger—sometimes progressing from something that could have taken a few hours, to something that now takes days. Or it could be a project that was supposed to take only a few days, and now weeks—or even months later—it's still creeping along to the finish line.

It happens. But sharing a set time line that spells out who should be completing specific tasks by specific dates, and holding people's feet to the fire about it, is crucial to managing what you're delegating—but without micromanaging.

Epilogue

Establishing a clear timeline, communicating it, and monitoring progress toward it, is crucial to delegating success.

121

Follow Up

Your work doesn't end after you've handed out responsibilities and tasks. In fact, it's just beginning. Following up with your employees—and finding the right balance of follow-up—is key to successfully delegating.

Follow-up should be something you've established when you set expectations, meaning you've made it clear that you'll be holding regular one-on-one sessions with each employee about how he is progressing.

These follow-up meetings help you keep tabs on what's been accomplished; what barriers the employee might be facing, particularly if collaborating with another division or a difficult coworker; what coaching the employee needs; and so forth. They also allow you an opportunity, or enhanced opportunity, to build a stronger rapport with your team members. In fact, social psychology research has found that mere exposure builds trust and likeability. So, in addition to keeping progress on track, you give yourself and your employee an opportunity to build a stronger rapport and a better working relationship.

But follow-up has to be that—follow-up, and not micromanaging. If you're hovering over your employ-

> **Assignment**
>
> Hold regular follow-up meetings to keep employees and projects on track.

ee or questioning every move, you'll be resented. To avoid this from happening, set follow-up meetings weekly, depending on the task or responsibility. Then use that time to listen; let the employee lead the discussion and ask questions. Taking this approach, your comments and responses are more likely to be perceived as helpful guidance. And if everything is moving along on schedule and as expected, follow-up is a good time to give praise and encouragement.

Epilogue

Following up with whom you've delegated tasks or responsibilities is a critical monitoring system, but also an opportunity to build rapport, provide coaching, and encourage your employees.

122

Confidence in Competence

Assuming you've done the employee assessment discussed earlier, you should have confidence in the competency of the people you've selected to take on the designated tasks and responsibilities.

But that may not be the case with the employee. Don't be surprised if you get push-back from an employee about taking on a given job. And don't take that push-back as a sign the employee is refusing or trying to wiggle her way out of work. Your employee could suffer from a lack of confidence in his own competency in a certain skill set or job knowledge.

When assigning tasks or responsibilities, review the employee's accomplishments with her, and be very clear about why you believe that history of success makes her the best person to take on the role you have in mind. You can also use it as an opportunity to show how the task or responsibility will enhance his existing competency.

Assignment

Explain why you chose the employee for the delegated task, making it clear what he can both gain and give from and to the project.

Also, acknowledge what skills the employee may be short on. This is not to emphasize the shortcomings, but rather to assure the employee that you have reasonable expectations of him and realize that finance, for example, may not be his forte. But nonetheless, you believe he can successfully accomplish the task based on the skills and knowledge he brings to the job. Follow-up meetings will allow you to give continued encouragement and reinforce your confidence in him.

Epilogue

Delegating, founded on thorough employee assessment and with regular follow-up, can help to build an employee's confidence in himself—making him ready to tackle more challenging projects down the road.

123

Fight the Fear of Mistrust

Just as you may have to fight the fear of giving up power with delegation, you may also have to fight the fear of mistrust. If you don't, you'll find yourself micromanaging instead of delegating.

Doing a thorough assessment of your team is the first step in being sure you've made the right decisions in determining to whom you should delegate which responsibilities. If you've taken the time to assess and given it quality thought, you should be able to stop second-guessing yourself. You've made the best decision with the best information you have available. No one could do more.

Assignment

Dig down underneath your feelings of mistrust and pinpoint what is stirring that nagging, gnawing feeling. It could be a lack of trust in your own judgment.

But if you find yourself still having feelings of mistrust even after you've done your homework in assessing your team, ask yourself why. Are there any facts or observations about the person that supports your mistrust? Or is it just a strong intuition?

Of course we all have to go with the gut sometimes, so don't dismiss a strong intuition, either. If you truly don't trust someone's capabilities, attitude, or loyalty, then don't delegate to him. You'll find yourself watching over his shoulder and doubting your own judgment.

But if your mistrust stems from your lack of confidence in your ability to delegate properly, then start small. Break the project down into manageable portions and give them out in succession, assigning the next task after the first has been

150

completed to your satisfaction. This step-by-step approach will help to build your confidence in your employee and your own judgment.

Epilogue

A thorough team assessment helps you fight the fear of mistrust in your employees.

124

The Big Decisions

Handing off the smaller tasks that have limited affect is easy, but what about the big decisions, such as managing the project budget or hiring an outside consultant? Is that something you should delegate?

Assignment

When delegating the bigger decisions, don't be afraid—just do your homework in selecting the right delegates.

It depends. Remember, how you decide to delegate authority is different from how you decide to delegate responsibilities. And when you delegate the big decisions, you're delegating some of your authority.

Delegating authority means you're handing over a whole set of responsibilities. You can't just hand that over to anyone. It has to be someone who you trust in competency and character. That is a person you know, beyond a reasonable doubt, that will think like you think, and in whom you have confidence regarding knowledge and judgment.

> ### Epilogue
> *Delegating the bigger decisions means delegating some of your authority, and that requires a careful strategy in determining who is best for the job.*

125

Fight the Fear of Delegating the Bigger Decisions

Just as it is easy to delegate the small, low-impact tasks or responsibilities, it is also easy to give in to the fear of delegating larger decisions.

Learning to delegate is fraught with fears. In fact, it can feel like a minefield of fear. Everywhere you turn, you see something that could blow up. And going wrong when delegating the bigger decisions can set off a chain reaction that could land you in the unemployment line.

> ### Assignment
>
> To get over your fear of delegating the bigger decisions, put them in perspective and start conquering them one step at a time.

So, you should proceed with caution when rolling the big dice. But proceeding with caution can still move you forward. If you find yourself holding onto the big decisions, and that is holding you back from achieving greater success, then get some perspective. Or better stated, put big decisions in perspective.

What do you consider big decisions? Make a list. Then label them A, B, C, and so on. Start at the very bottom of the list and ask yourself if this big decision is small enough to give to your most trusted team member. If so, then take the leap—by sharing your vision, setting expectations, and following up.

Epilogue

When it comes to delegating the bigger decisions, you may have to do it trembling, but by God, do it! Just do it right!

126

Outline Specifically What You Want Done

To help avoid the fears and second-guessing that can come with delegation, make a list that combines your expectations and the time line of when you expect them to be met. This is sometimes called mapping. But whatever it is called, it is a good idea for anyone who delegates—beginners or those veterans who just want to improve at it.

Outlining how you want an employee to tackle a delegated task or responsibility, or a big decision, provides a documented "schematic"—a road map going forward, a checklist along the way, and a reference for the future.

An outline of what you specifically want done can also serve as a guide for your follow-up meetings, giving those discussions both a framework and focal

Assignment

Create an outline that specifically lays out your expectations and a time line to keep your employees on track.

point. In short, use it as your agenda for keeping those discussions focused on progress, not failure.

Epilogue

Every good plan needs a road map, and a delegation outline can do just that in getting your team where it needs to go.

127

Spread the Word

Along with setting expectations with individual employees, you also need to set expectations with other team members and those that interact with your team. This will help to avoid conflict and unnecessary barriers once the employee begins to carry out the delegated task or responsibility.

Researchers have found that despite popular belief, it is not personalities or styles that are at the root of conflict in organizations. Instead, it is role ambiguity and role encroachment that sparks most territorial fires in-house.

When roles are unclear, people can unintentionally collide. And when it happens to rivals on a team, it can be like flint hitting rock. Sparks fly! The same can happen when role encroachment occurs. Just think of driving in traffic and a car arbitrarily weaves into your lane, cutting you off. That's a recipe for road rage—or worse. That same frustration can be played out in the workplace when roles are not clear.

To keep the internal traffic moving smoothly, be sure to spread the word about what you've delegated, to whom, and why. Consider it part of setting expectations. You expect others to respect the role you've assigned to an individual employee and to work collaboratively or cooperatively, depending on the situation, as the designee carries out that role.

But don't stop with your immediate team. If others in the organization will be affected by the decision

> ### *Assignment*
>
> Be sure to inform others of what you've delegated to whom and why.

you've made, be sure to inform them as well. This tells others the designee has your support and backing. Others will be less likely to act as possible road blocks if they understand the employee is not acting arbitrarily.

> ### Epilogue
> *Explaining what and why you've delegated will greatly reduce the risks of conflict within your immediate team and in other areas of the organization.*

128

Don't Jump at the First Sign of Trouble

When toddlers are learning to walk, parents learn quickly to hang back when they stumble. Children tend to right themselves and get back on course.

The same is true when delegating to others. If you see smoke, don't immediately assume there is fire. Jumping to the rescue too soon can dampen an employee's confidence in himself, and spark what could become smoldering resentment toward you.

So how do you hold back when you fear success could be in danger? Think expectations, time line, and follow-up. Call it the ABCs, or rather the ETFs, of delegation. When setting expectations, be clear on what you want done and how you generally would like it to be done. As part of that, explain how you would like to see concerns handled, at what stage you would like to know about them, and to what detail. But also ask the employee to bring one or two possible solutions to you as well.

If you're following up at regular intervals, you'll likely head off most problems before they arise.

Assignment

Use the EFT approach. It allows employees to be proactive in bringing problems and solutions to you according to your expectations, enabling them to save face, and demonstrate they can right themselves and get back on course. Not only will this sustain their confidence in themselves, it will also enhance their confidence in you as a steadfast, nonreactive leader.

Epilogue

If you follow the ETFs of delegation—expectations, time line, and follow-up—you will help your employees tackle concerns before they become problems, without the boss stepping in.

129

Continue to Move Forward Even When Problems Arise

Poet and author Maya Angelou once said, "There are no mistakes, only lessons." If you're going to be successful at delegating, you must have this attitude. It is not an option; it is mandatory.

No one, and no situation, is perfect. And in fact, imperfection can lead to some amazing discoveries. Think of penicillin, for example. Obstacles and failures can open doors that no one ever thought possible.

When problems arise regarding delegated work, think of them as lessons or opportunities. It could be a lesson that provides insight into an employee's approach to interacting with others, or a lesson to you that you need to communicate more clearly and specifically.

Or the problem could be an opportunity. In multinational manufacturing organizations, when a problem arises in one plant, it can be the result of a flawed process. And it is likely that process is followed in all other plants around the world. Detecting it in one can save the company millions of dollars in lost product—or even better, workers' or consumers' lives.

Assignment

Just as you'll need to move on from successful and failed decisions, you will also need to learn from problems that arise in delegating work, too.

If you help your employees see the lesson or opportunity in the problem, and guide them in overcoming it, they will have greater confidence in their ability to recover from setbacks and move forward.

Epilogue

When you see opportunity to learn and grow in problems with delegation, you give yourself and your team the chance to become better and wiser.

130

Have Employees Help Resolve Problems

If you have been following the advice in this book up until now, you have discovered that leaders who delegate well work collaboratively with their employees, empowering them and maintaining a dialogue throughout the process.

So what better partner to have in a dialogue than someone who is closest to the work, and the problems that go with it? After all, your employees are on the front line. They can see what is coming at them and can often see why or how.

Tap into this expertise, by all means! Don't let where someone sits in the organizational chart prevent you from seeking their input.

When setting expectations for the delegated task, make it clear that you want your employee to bring solutions to the table, and that you value her input on how the problems should be addressed.

Assignment

Tap into your employees' front line expertise to help resolve problems. Let them know you value their input.

One leader in a Midwest pharmaceutical company has a banner outside her door that says: "Got solution?" She expects that employees who bring a problem to her have some options in hand to resolve it. She may not always agree with their suggestions, but their opinions lead every conversation about resolving problems.

Epilogue

Leaders who delegate well work collaboratively with their employees—even in solving problems.

131

Perfection Not Necessary

Perfectionists beware! You could find delegation difficult. If you delegate with the expectation that everything will be done precisely as you've planned and directed, you're setting yourself up for disappointment.

> ### *Assignment*
>
> If you're prone to perfection, change your perception. Strive for excellence instead. After all, perfection is much like beauty—it is in the eye of the beholder.

If you're going to delegate, you're going to have to cast perfection to the wayside and instead focus on what success looks like. If the delegate achieves the results you want, and does it ethically and within the parameters of the law and company policy, then chalk it up to a win. It's okay if there are a few minor bumps and glitches along the way. They build character—and hone problem-solving skills.

And if you're someone who holds to the viewpoint that "if you want anything done right, you better do it yourself," you're going to need an attitude adjustment to be successful at delegation. Let's face it; no one will do things exactly as you would do them. In fact, it's diverse thinking and styles that often make the strongest teams.

Epilogue
When delegating, cast perfection aside and aim for excellence instead.

132

Organizational Rewards of Delegating

When you delegate well, you deliver a whole range of benefits to your organization.

First, the organization gets more from you, such as better use of your skills and talents, better prioritization, better decision making, and better stewardship of its resources.

The organization also gets smarter results. By leveraging the diverse expertise, talents, skills, and creativity of your team members, you can find better ways to approach projects, or tackle recurring problems that could affect other areas of the organization.

Ultimately, your company also gets smarter, more competent employees. In the end, delegation helps to make an organization more efficient and effective. And what CEO or business owner could refuse those rewards?

> ### *Assignment*
>
> See delegating as offering someone an opportunity to develop and grow, to hone her skills and knowledge, and channel that refined competency back into making the organization stronger and better.

Epilogue
Delegation delivers a number of returns to the organization, such as smarter management, more competent, focused employees, and more efficient and effective operations.

133

Your Rewards for Delegating

The list of what you can gain personally and professionally from delegation is long.

At the top of the list is a sense of relief from being over-loaded, overworked, and overwhelmed. Coping with these feelings over an extended period of time can lead to all kinds of health and emotional issues. They can also dull your thinking, your enthusiasm, and your dedication. But delegation can be the antidote.

Also on the list is an engaged, focused team that runs like a well-oiled machine to the point you just have to wind it up and let it go (keeping the ETFs in mind, of course). Good delegation can reward you with a team that is engaged, empowered, loyal, capable, and focused on results. For you that means a sense of accomplishment each day and a healthy self-esteem for all.

Assignment

Take account of the immediate and long-term rewards you can get from delegating successfully.

These are the rewards of true leaders, those who know how to unite people, bring out the best in them, and channel their talents, energies, and expertise in a collective direction. Yes! Delegation, done right, can help do all that!

Epilogue
Delegation, done well, can reap personal and profes-sional rewards that go far beyond—and outlive—the fleeting pleasures of a promotion or pay raise.

161

134

You Get Relieved of Workload

Ever had that gnawing feeling that wakes you at 2 a.m., sending you bolt upright in a cold sweat, with your to-do list running frantically through your mind? If you have, you know it can be anxiety at its best—or worst.

If you're experiencing the 2 a.m. jolt, you're likely suffering from a case of the three Os: overworked, overloaded, and overwhelmed. Dealing with them individually can be stressful, but dealing with them in combination can be paralyzing.

Delegation can sooth this ailment.

One of the key rewards of delegation is relief from the three Os. Sharing the workload among your team members can be like opening a release valve, relieving you of pent-up pressure that can dull your thinking and diminish your decision making.

> **Assignment**
>
> Instead of being knee-deep in tasks, use delegation to share opportunity and practice your leadership skills of planning, monitoring, and coaching your team to success.

And when you use delegation to let go of that pressure, you turn it into opportunity for others around you. In short, your relief could be someone else's chance to shine, grow, and learn.

> **Epilogue**
> *Delegation can relieve you of the day-to-day workload, freeing you up to refine your leadership skills.*

135

Greater Team Involvement

When you delegate effectively, you turn employees into team players. You give them each a piece of the action, a chance to get on the court and play, show their stuff, and share in the victory.

You also give them a chance for insight and input. Because effective delegation demands follow-up and open communication between you and your employees, your team members get a direct line into your thinking, what you want to accomplish, and how you want it accomplished. Believe it or not, all employees want this. They want to know how to please the boss, and how they can be part of the bigger picture.

But delegation also gives you access to your very own think tank—your employees! Encouraging their input as part of completing their delegated tasks and responsibilities gives you access to scores of ideas and solutions. When you get into the swing of delegating regularly, you'll find you no longer have to sit in solitude wracking your brain for answers.

> ### *Assignment*
>
> Tap into your employees' thoughts—and save yourself wear and tear on your own mind, and nerves.

Epilogue

Delegation provides a ready-made opportunity to get your team involved, allowing you to better connect with your employees and tap into their collective brain power.

136

Better Results

In delegating, you give your employees skin in the game. You align them with a higher purpose—the big picture. When you share your vision with your employees, and then help them understand how a delegated task or responsibility can contribute to the bigger picture, you set the stage for better results.

And practicing the ETFs of delegation ensures you get those better results. By setting expectations, you make it clear what you want the end game to look like. In establishing a time line, you make it clear when you want those results to come to fruition, and when you regularly follow up, you get to see the process of those results blossoming from expectations into reality.

When employees are included in achieving the big picture through delegation, they are much more likely to be dedicated to the end game. And they are less likely to be distracted or deterred by potential problems and barriers. Instead, they tend to be more hopeful, more confident, and more committed.

Assignment

Use delegation to help encourage dedication to better results as a whole.

Epilogue

By delegating, you give your employees skin in the game, and ownership in achieving the overall purpose, which contributes to better results in the end.

137

Increased Team Loyalty

Got a team that bickers and gossips? If so, delegation can help curb this behavior—or keep your team from developing it.

A team that squabbles and gossips is in need of engaging work, better focus, and collective commitment to a larger purpose. Delegation can help to fill these needs and bring your team together as a loyal, smart-working, confident, and dedicated group.

When you're sharing the workload, you're ensuring others have enough to do. And by assessing the team thoroughly, as part of delegating effectively, you can ensure you're assigning work that is challenging and thought provoking according to each employee's skill level and development needs.

Assignment

Team loyalty is a natural result of engaging, but challenging work that gets people focused and contributing to a higher mission. You can give your team all of these by learning how to delegate.

Effective delegation also requires that you make it clear who is assigned which tasks and responsibilities, avoiding role ambiguity and role encroachment—the top reasons for conflict in organizations. Delegation also helps to unite your employees, again giving them a stake in the larger purpose of the work at hand.

Epilogue

Create a loyal, smart-working, confident, and dedicated team through effective delegation.

138

Enhanced Capabilities

When marketers determine pricing for an organization's products, they take into account workers' capabilities in manufacturing that product and factor in the workforce's efficiency. But as workers become better at producing the product through time, pricing will start to fall, as the company can manufacture higher volumes of product at an increasingly more efficient rate.

Confusing? Okay, let's take an example from the computer industry. A decade ago, it was not unusual to pay $2,500 for a basic desktop computer. Today, you can find quality desktop computers with significantly more features and memory than their predecessors—and for less than $600. Why? The industry's workforce has increased its capabilities in manufacturing personal computers to the point where they are efficient enough to produce more at the same, or less, cost than they did a decade ago.

> ### *Assignment*
>
> When you delegate, you give your employees the opportunity to become more capable. As they routinely stretch and flex their capability muscles over time, the more efficient and valuable they become to you and to the organization.

As a result, the computer industry is now able to offer computers at a more affordable price, so that more people can afford to buy them. And that means higher sales revenue and potentially higher profits.

The point is that as people are exposed to new ways of working and become more capable over time, they bring greater value to the company—and can even help it expand into new markets.

Epilogue

Delegation creates enhanced capabilities, and that can translate into organizational rewards in the short- and long-term future.

139

Enhanced Self-Esteem

One of the greatest rewards of delegation is improved self-esteem—for you and your employees. Self-esteem can be a double-edged sword. When it's high, much is possible. But when it's low, it can do a lot of damage.

Self-esteem can either buoy people to new heights of achievement or, when it's lacking, can hold them back from using their talents and living up to their highest potential. Erma Bombeck once said, "When I stand before God at the end of my life, I would hope that I would not have a single bit of talent left, and could say, 'I used everything you gave me.'"

When you delegate engaging and challenging work to your employees, you give them the opportunity to live up to their potential. Each time your employees succeed in a delegated task or responsibility, they get a chance to affirm their own abilities and worth.

As a leader, you get the same opportunity. Each time you delegate effective-

> **Assignment**
>
> Use delegation to plant the seeds of greatness in your employees, and then cultivate them.

ly, and lead an employee to success, you confirm your leadership skills both for yourself, with your team members, and with your superiors and peers.

Epilogue

Each time your employees succeed in a delegated task or responsibility, they get a chance to affirm their own abilities and worth. Each time you lead an employee to success with a delegated task, you confirm your leadership skills to yourself and those around you.

140

Enhanced Sense of Accomplishment

Accomplishments, individually, are the building blocks of great things—and a true sense of fulfillment.

Just as each task completed successfully leads to a sustained, healthy self-esteem, the same is true with day-to-day accomplishments. But it starts with a vision, a snapshot of a bigger picture, a higher purpose or mission. And good delegation provides this from the start.

Assignment

Use each accomplishment to build confidence and encourage employees to keep moving ahead toward the ultimate goal.

When employees are focused on a common goal or purpose, they are less likely to fall victim to days filled with frenetic activity and, instead, channel their thinking, energy, and teamwork in one collective direction. This, when framed with clear expectations, time lines, and open communication with each other and the boss, creates fertile ground for accomplishment.

168

In delegating effectively, you give employees a clear picture of what you're all working toward, how and what you want accomplished, and the time frame in which you want it done. And every follow-up conversation gives you an opportunity to note large and small accomplishments along the way.

Epilogue

Accomplishments, both large and small, are the building blocks of great things—and ultimately lead to a true sense of fulfillment.

141

The Importance of Trust

Booker T. Washington once said, "Few things help an individual more than to place responsibility upon him, and to let him know that you trust him."

This is never more true than when delegating to someone. In fact, trust is a core principle of good delegation. Yes, trusting someone with key responsibilities, tasks, and authority means taking some risk. But all businesses face some risk—it can't be avoided. Yet, if you follow the ETFs of delegation, you can greatly reduce the risks involved and venture to trust those around you.

And showing someone that you trust him can be like a spark that fuels his motivation and gets him moving in the right direction. Think about a time when someone put her trust in you with a special task. Didn't it feel good to know that someone had confidence in you? Didn't you strive to give your very best, because he believed in you?

When you trust your employees to carry out delegated tasks and responsibilities, you give them much more than direction and work. You show them you believe in them. And that kind of investment can garner returns

> ### *Assignment*
>
> Remember this! The effects of good delegation really can be profound.

that are sometimes beyond measure in people's lives.

> ### Epilogue
> *Trust is a core principle of good delegation, and showing people you trust them can be like lighting a spark that fuels their motivation and gets them moving in the right direction.*

142

Provide Training

Okay, you've done your team assessment and established your expectations, but you're still feeling uneasy about turning a team member loose with the task.

It happens. In fact, this is where the rubber meets the road in defining leaders from managers. Good leaders ensure their people are always set up to succeed. But how do you do that? Charles Merrill, Founder of Merrill Lynch, said it best: "Get the best people and train them well."

Sometimes employees need some form of training before they can launch full-steam ahead. That can be either formal or informal training. Some people learn best by taking a class or working through an online program, while others learn best by watching and practicing.

However, some tasks require more formalized education. This is why it is so important to assess your team and have a game plan (see Idea 114) in place before you delegate. Both processes help you think through factors such as training, education, and so

> ### *Assignment*
>
> In the end, it is up to you to ensure your employees have the tools they need to properly complete the job you have assigned to them.

forth. If an employee will need further formal education, it could take some time before she is properly knowledgeable and prepared to take on the task.

> ### Epilogue
> *Good leaders ensure their people are always set up to succeed. When delegating, follow the advice of Charles Merrill: "Get the best people <u>and train them well</u>."*

143

Training for Trouble

So what do you do when the project you've delegated is moving along nicely, and then your employee leading it hits a patch where he is out of his league in terms of knowledge or expertise?

If coaching during follow-up sessions does not help, and you see your employee struggling or becoming frustrated, you need to step in and determine if additional training is needed.

It is important not to let your employee's frustration override his confidence. Take matters into hand immediately. But work together with your employee to determine the best course of action. For example, does he need to attend a formal training on a specific topic, or would riding along with a sales representative for a week give him the insight and knowledge he needs?

Sometimes mere exposure is enough to help round out the rough edges when an employee hits a difficult patch.

Assignment

Working with your employee to determine where he is struggling can help bring the best solution to light. Partnering in this vein also will allow your employee to maintain ownership of the task, and help keep his confidence in tact.

But it could take time in a formal training program, instead.

Epilogue

Be prepared to step back and provide training if an employee finds himself struggling along the way. Taking this step quickly is important to avoid letting your employee's frustration override his self-confidence.

144

Celebrate Success

Look for opportunities to recognize your employees publicly when they meet your expectations with the delegated tasks and responsibilities.

This could be something ranging from a team award to a pat on the back in front of *your* boss. But take the time to find out how your employee likes to be recognized for a job well done. Some people feel embarrassed by group displays of appreciation, and some just aren't particularly motivated by money. In fact, the overachievers in your group are more likely to be motivated by being given even more responsibility and challenge. But if you ask each employee when you're establishing expectations, the E in the ETFs of delegation, you'll know for certain—and then you can put it to use.

And don't just wait for the big accomplishments. Celebrate even the small victories along the way. Good leaders look for reasons to applaud their employees, even if it's just for having a good attitude.

Assignment

It is the small steps that add up to the big ones, so look for ways to recognize your employees as they progress in completing their delegated tasks and responsibilities.

Epilogue

When delegating, remember the words of business guru Tom Peters: "Celebrate what you want to see more of."

145

Reward Success

In the process of celebrating success, reward it! Some organizations budget to reward success, such as through a bonus program or merit pay increases. Others encourage their leaders to give more nominal rewards, such as movie tickets or a day off.

Nonprofits and government organizations sometimes have to find other means of rewarding their employees due to shoestring budgets and ethical policies.

Michele, a supervisor working for a government agency in the Midwest has her hands tied by state policy when it comes to giving employees a bonus or even taking them to lunch on the agency's dime. So, she looks for other ways to reward and recognize, such as a round high-five from the team during a staff meeting to acknowledge someone's good performance. Or she leaves employees voice mails to start their day, recognizing them for a job well done, and she mails them cards with words of praise for a specific achievement.

Assignment

Learn what types of performance incentives are available through your organization, and then put your imagination to work rewarding success!

However, almost all organizations have a performance review process, and that presents a great opportunity to reward success. That reward can be either in words of praise that goes into the person's personnel file for the future, or if the success is consistent over time or significant, it could warrant a pay increase.

Epilogue
Reward employees when they are successful at delegated tasks and responsibilities.

146

Be Encouraging

Your encouragement is the crucial fuel to keep your team chugging along in the right direction. We often think it is discipline that keeps people on the straight and narrow, but as German poet Johann Wolfgang Von Goethe once said: "Correction does much, but encouragement does more."

For delegation to be successful, you must encourage your team—day in and day out. Celebrating and rewarding success are also necessary, but to get there people often must be encouraged through the bumps and bruises they experience along the way. For example, encourage your employee when he has weathered a rough interaction with a tough colleague. Or help a frustrated employee look back and see how far she's come with a project or task.

Assignment

The philosopher Ovid once said, "the spirited horse, which will try to win the race of its own accord, will run even faster if encouraged." The translation of that is simple: If you invest in the day-to-day care and concern for your team, they will work harder and more intelligently, and they will give you their respect and loyalty that will last for years.

Encouragement does cost you, however. It costs you time, listening, compassion, understanding, and caring. But the investment can reap huge rewards.

Epilogue
Encouragement is the day-to-day fuel that drives your team to success in the end.

147

Be More Than a Good Listener

Though it's highly underrated in our American culture, listening is the most powerful tool of leadership—and it is absolutely necessary at all stages of the delegation process. But it is particularly important in your efforts to encourage your staff.

Few people would turn away a chance to have the boss truly listen to their ideas and concerns. After all, it's a chance to be understood by the very person that determines their livelihood—and all people, in even the smallest things, want to be understood.

But the type of listening that makes delegation successful goes beyond the traditional steps of hearing, asking questions for clarity, affirming what you've heard, and then responding. To successfully delegate, you need to become an *engaged* listener. That means getting to know your employees, know what makes them tick, what concerns them, and what their aspirations are. Get to know how they came to be on your team, and where they want to go in the future. In essence, have a conversation with them.

> ### Assignment
>
> Be an engaged listener through every step of the delegation process.

Being an engaged listener requires you to get to know people as people, and not merely delegates for the work at hand. Not only will the time and energy you invest be an encouragement to your employees, but you'll also gain knowledge and rapport that will pay off long after the delegated task is completed.

Epilogue

Screenwriter Wilson Mizner has good advice for delegating managers: "A good listener is not only popular everywhere, but after awhile he gets to know something."

148

Be a Mentor

We can all thank Homer for giving us Mentor, a character in his epic tale *The Odyssey*, who personifies that relationship where hindsight, insight, and foresight often are passed from the older and wiser to the younger and less experienced.

We all need mentors in our lives. Sometimes they are grandparents or older family members, a teacher or college professor, or a colleague that knows the ropes and can help us learn them, too. Whoever a mentor may be in a given situation, we need them both personally and professionally.

Assignment

All you have to do is listen, encourage, coach, and listen, encourage and coach, and—well, you get the idea.

And each time you delegate a task, you have the opportunity to mentor someone. You don't have to assign any official labels to it, or make a formal announcement that you'll now be "mentoring" your staff.

When you set expectations at the onset of delegation, you have an opportunity to mentor. When you empower your employees to develop solutions and solve problems, you have an opportunity to mentor. When you hold regular follow-up sessions to monitor the delegated task, you have an opportunity to mentor.

177

> **Epilogue**
> *Mentoring is a natural part of delegating effectively.*

149

Be a Resource

Go beyond being a source of work assignments and, instead, become a resource for your employees.

That means you not only make information available, but you actively seek it out and readily share it with others. You also align that information with your team members' development ment needs and delegated assignments. Being a resource means you act as a well of knowledge that others can go to when they have questions, or just want to know more on a particular topic.

And no, that does not mean you have to have all the answers to all the questions.

Being a resource simply means having enough

> ### *Assignment*
>
> Build and maintain a catalogue of information and a network of knowledgeable professionals to help you set up your team to succeed in the tasks and responsibilities you delegate to them.

knowledge to lead people to the answers. Perhaps you know of a good book or course that can give more insight and information on a particular topic. If you belong to a professional organization, you can share publications and articles with your team to expose them to other voices in the industry on an issue they are dealing with—or need to be ready to deal with down the road.

Or maybe you know of someone, or someone who knows someone, who works in a specific field and would be willing to share her expertise with your employees.

Epilogue

You don't have to have all the answers to be a resource; you simply need to have enough knowledge to lead people to the answers.

150

Don't Delegate and Forget!

If you've made it this far in the book, then you know that delegation is a pretty big responsibility—and it requires so much more from you than merely handling out work assignments.

Delegation is about taking charge of yourself, your priorities, your time, your management style, your reactions, and your resources. And it's implementing deci-

Assignment

Remember this! In the grander scheme of life, delegation is about growing yourself and those around you—challenging all to reach, stretch, and come closer with each opportunity to live up to their fullest potential.

sions intelligently, and in a way that compounds your team's effectiveness and efficiency for future projects and tasks.

So, when you delegate, don't just doll out responsibilities; remember that you need a game plan that describes the vision, shows others how they can contribute to it, aligns team talents and interests with the work at hand, sets expectations, keeps people on task, and creates opportunity for dialogue that builds rapport and team loyalty along the way.

Epilogue

Delegation is about implementing decisions in a way that grows yourself and others—and your organization.

151

Make Delegation a Standard Operating Procedure

If you haven't already started to put the delegation techniques described here into practice yet, what are you waiting for? Your team is depending on you, and so is you organization.

Start taking the steps outlined in this book to first make better decisions, and then to implement them effectively through delegation. The more you practice them, the better you'll become through time. If you haven't started trying them on for size already, the clock is ticking and opportunity is passing you by.

Practice the delegation techniques each day, in small increments, until they become a habit. Within weeks you'll find you're getting more done, with better results, and with better relationships to boot. If you follow the path laid out among these pages, throughout the next

Assignment

Remember, delegation is about uniting people, talents, skills, and knowledge to work smarter, not harder.

few months you'll find that you've made delegating effectively a standard operating procedure in how you get work done.

Epilogue

Delegation takes practice, but if you take the time and make the effort, you'll find over time it will become a standard operating procedure in working smarter.

Index

About the Authors

Robert E. Dittmer, APR

Bob Dittmer has more than 35 years experience in public relations, marketing, and higher education.

He currently serves as a faculty member of the Indiana University School of Journalism, culminating more than 15 years as an adjunct faculty member with colleges and universities around the country in both graduate and undergraduate programs. He teaches public relations courses, is responsible for managing the public relations sequence, and serves as the marketing and retention officer for the school.

He also has served as the director of media relations for both an American government organization with responsibilities for all of Europe, as well as for a major NATO organization with responsibilities for public information worldwide. Bob has more than 15 years experience in public relations and advertising agencies, working with a wide variety of clients in both business-to-business and business-to-consumer arenas. He is also an author and literary agent.

With a B.A. from John Carroll University, an M.A. from Marshall University, and accreditation from the Public Relations Society of America (PRSA), he is also dedicated to his profession. He was the 1998 president of the Hoosier (Indiana) Chapter, PRSA. He also served as 1999 chair of PRSA's National Association Section and as chair of PRSA's East Central District in 2001 (five states) and remains on the Board of Directors of the Hoosier Chapter. Bob was elected to membership in the Indianapolis Public Relations Society in 1998.

Bob has spent years managing governmental and business units worldwide, including owning his own consultancy. Throughout the years he has collected the experiences, thoughts, and ideas he and others have developed to solve the management challenges we all face daily. He is the author of *151 Quick Ideas to Manage Your Time*. He is currently at work cowriting another book on writing.

Bob and his wife, Susan, live in Indianapolis.

Stephanie M. McFarland, APR

Stephanie McFarland's management career began more than 20 years ago, supervising employees for her family's business. While most 16-year-olds were "hanging out," she was home doing payroll to ensure employees could receive their paychecks on Friday.

Through the past 18 years, Stephanie has managed projects, teams, and departments in multinational, Fortune 500, government, consultancy, and nonprofit organizations. She had provided public relations management counseling to more than 20 clients and employers in industries ranging from electric utilities to pharmaceuticals. Her personal philosophy of management has evolved over the years from merely culling employees to "get the job done," to discovering what makes them tick and seeking out ways to develop them for their current roles and beyond.

Stephanie is a certified crisis consultant and an accredited public relations professional with the Public Relations Society of America. She holds her B.A. in English from Indiana University and her master's of science in communication management from Syracuse University in New York.

In addition, Stephanie is an adjunct faculty member of the Indiana University School of Journalism in Indianapolis, where she teaches public relations management courses to undergraduate and graduate students.

Her management experience has earned her numerous awards in advertising and public relations.

She lives just outside of Indianapolis with her husband, 6-year-old daughter, and their two dogs, Sebastian and Baxter.